STUDYING *The Lord of the Rings*

Anna Dawson

Contents

The Lord of the Rings Factsheet

The Fellowship of the Ring

Running Time	178 minutes
Certificate	PG
Release Date	16 December 2001

Synopsis

Bilbo, a hobbit of the Shire, has in his possession the One Ring, forged by the Dark Lord Sauron, capable of allowing him to return to full strength and rule Middle Earth. At his 111th birthday party, advised by the wizard Gandalf, he gives the Ring to nephew Frodo, who sets off with his companions Sam, Pippin and Merry to take the Ring out of the Shire. After Gandalf is betrayed by his superior, Saruman, the hobbits are guided by Aragorn (the exiled King of Gondor) towards the Elven haven Rivendell. On the way Frodo is stabbed by a Black Rider, footsoldiers of Sauron. He is rescued and at Rivendell a Fellowship of nine is formed to take the Ring to Mount Doom in Mordor, the only place where it can be destroyed. Along the way Gandalf falls during a battle in the Mines of Moria, and as Saruman breeds a savage army of Urak Hai at Isengard the Fellowship begins to splinter, as predicted by the wise elf, Galadriel. Eventually Boromir tries to take the Ring from Frodo who escapes just as Urak Hai attack. Boromir is mortally wounded, Pippin and Merry are taken captive, and Aragorn slays the Urak responsible for wounding Boromir, who dies redeemed. Frodo leaves the Fellowship behind to journey to Mordor with the Ring, accompanied by Sam.

The Two Towers

Running Time	179 minutes
Certificate	12A
Release Date	18 December 2002

Synopsis

Lost, Sam and Frodo scale the rocks of Emyn Muil on their way to Mordor. Meanwhile Aragorn, the elf Legolas and the dwarf Gimli track the captive Merry and Pippin and on their way meet Éomer. The people of Rohan are terrorised by Saruman. Frodo and Sam capture the creature Gollum, who agrees to take them to Mordor, Aragorn and company track Merry and Pippin into Fangorn Forest, where, from a resurrected Gandalf the White, they learn they are safe with Treebeard and the Ents. They set off for Edoras in Rohan, and release King Theoden from Saruman's spell. There Aragorn meets Éowyn who falls in love with him. The people of Rohan flee to Helm's Deep.

Frodo and Sam arrive at the Black Gate of Mordor but are persuaded by Gollum to enter by another route. They are captured by Faramir of Gondor (Boromir's brother) who discovers from Gollum that they carry the Ring. He takes them to Gondor. Meanwhile the people of Rohan are attacked on their way to Helm's Deep by Saruman's wargs, and Aragorn falls from a cliff. He recovers and sets off for Helm's Deep where he sees an army of 10,000 Urak Hai marching towards it. As Merry and Pippin try to engage the Ents in the conflict, the battle for Helm's Deep begins. It is seemingly hopeless until Gandalf arrives with Éomer and the Rohirrim, at the same time that the Ents realise Saruman's treachery and destroy Isengard. The battle of Helm's Deep won and Isengard destroyed, Frodo and Sam are led by Gollum towards Mordor. He is plotting to have them killed, and take the Ring for himself.

The Return of the King

Running Time	201 minutes
Certificate	12A
Release Date	17 December 2003

Synopsis

Frodo and Sam continue to be led by a treacherous Gollum while Aragorn and companions celebrate the victories at Helm's Deep and Isengard. Pippin looks into Saruman's seeing stone and sees Sauron's plan to attack Minas Tirith, the city of Gondor, so he and Gandalf ride to warn them. Sam discovers Gollum's plotting but is not believed by Frodo who is increasingly under the influence of the Ring. On her way to leave Middle Earth, Arwen sees a vision of her son with Aragorn and turns back, encouraging her father to reforge Isildur's sword. In Gondor, Gandalf and Pippin meet with the Steward Denethor who is grieving for his son, Boromir. Frodo, Sam and Gollum reach Minas Morgul while Osgiliath in Gondor is attacked. Over-ruling Denethor, Gandalf has the beacons of Gondor lit and Rohan rides to their aid and to war.

The Lord of the Rings Factsheet

Gollum's scheming results in Frodo sending Sam away. Aragorn is visited by Elrond who gives him the reforged sword. He leaves for the Paths of the Dead after telling Éowyn that he cannot love her. Frodo is attacked by the giant spider, Shelob, and eventually stung after fighting with Gollum, who seems to have tumbled to his death. Sam then battles and defeats the spider but Frodo is taken away by orcs. Minas Tirith is under attack, as Pippin and Gandalf save Faramir who is being burned alive by his father, mad with grief. Aragorn persuades the Dead Army to fight for him, as King of Gondor. Outside Minas Tirith the Rohirrim arrive and the battle of Pelennor Fields commences. King Théoden is knocked from his horse by the lead Black Ringer, the Witch King, who Éowyn, having ridden to battle with Merry in disguise, kills. Aragorn arrives with the Dead Army and the battle is won.

Captured by orcs, an injured Frodo awakes in a tower, the Ring gone. Sam, who has the Ring, rescues him and they set off for Mount Doom. Meanwhile Aragorn plans to lead the army to the Black Gate and distract Sauron from Frodo's mission. Frodo and Sam finally reach Mount Doom and are confronted by Gollum. As Sauron's orc army begin to fight Aragorn, Frodo reaches the summit but is unable to bring himself to destroy the Ring. Gollum fights him for it and bites off his finger, joyous that he possesses the Ring at last, but falls to his death into Mount Doom with the Ring, which is finally destroyed. Frodo and Sam are rescued and reunited with the remaining Fellowship. Aragorn is crowned King of Gondor and reunited with Arwen. The hobbits return to the Shire where Sam marries his sweetheart. Finally Bilbo, Gandalf and Frodo depart with the Elves across the sea, leaving Middle Earth forever.

Key Credits

Director	Peter Jackson
Producers	Peter Jackson, Fran Walsh, Barry M. Osborne, Rick Porras
Executive Producers	Michael Lynne, Mark Ordesky, Robert Shaye, Bob and Harvey Weinstein
Screenplay	Peter Jackson, Fran Walsh, Phillippa Boyens
Cinematography	Andrew Lesnee
Music	Howard Shore
Production Companies	New Line, Wingnut Films
Distributor	Entertainment (UK)
Budget	$300m (approximately)

Cast

Frodo Baggins	Elijah Wood
Samwise Gamgee	Sean Astin
Gandalf	Ian McKellen
Aragorn/Strider	Viggo Mortensen
Legolas	Orlando Bloom
Gimli	John Rhys-Davies
Merry	Dominic Monaghan
Pippin	Billy Boyd
Gollum	Andy Serkis
Boromir	Sean Bean
Arwen	Liv Tyler
Éowyn	Miranda Otto
Galadriel	Cate Blanchett
Elrond	Hugo Weaving
Saruman	Christopher Lee
Théoden	Bernard Hill
Éomer	Karl Urban
Bilbo Baggins	Ian Holm
Faramir	David Wenham

Introduction

The Lord of the Rings films have undoubtedly become the most successful cinematic phenomenon since the original Star Wars trilogy (1977–83). Filmed concurrently, and released at Christmas over a three-year period with subsequent extended DVD releases for committed fans, the series of films has achieved what may to some have seemed unachievable, creating three critically and commercially vastly successful films with enough appeal to offer different audiences different experiences. With a theatrical box-office take alone of almost three billion US dollars, not to mention a clean sweep of eleven Oscars at the 2003 Academy Awards, it would appear that the one saga really did rule them all.

Made by a director then little-known to a wider public and filmed back-to-back in New Zealand, it was a project of enormous vision and financial gamble (which is easy to underplay in retrospect) that really hit the jackpot. Why was the series so successful? Was it that the detail and depth of narrative in the films were so beyond that normally served up by effects-driven contemporary blockbusters? Was it that the world represented on screen was familiar yet distanced enough to offer pure escapism and spectacular pleasures rounded with humanist melodrama and dazzling battle sequences? It appears the answers to these questions are as complex as the production of the films themselves, with no one element being easily decipherable without considering all. What is of particular interest about the films is that they utilised a highly strategic phenomenon of the blockbuster in terms of their marketing and distribution, yet harnessed the enthusiasm of devotees and won wide critical acceptance.

The aim of this Guide is to offer a way into looking at the films from the point of view of the major components of Film and Media Studies: their complex origins and narrative structure, their generic patterns, thematic concerns, issues of representation and the industrial elements of the films. These elements include looking at Jackson as New Hollywood auteur, institutions and audiences. Additionally there are sections considering the films as texts in detail from the point of view of the creation of diegetic 'realism' so vital for the films, analysing locations and settings, costume, weaponry and props, special effects, use of camera and editing, and sound and soundtrack. The aim in all sections is to highlight critical debates and key terms, to relate these to the films and to explore their stylistic and cultural impact.

It must be noted that this is *not* meant as a study guide to Tolkien's book, or to the adaptation process of page to screen, other than where it has implications for textual or institutional analysis of the films. There are many books and guides that look at the literary phenomenon. The concern of this Guide is the three films as texts and cultural products, based on their cinematic release forms (in other words not in their extended DVD versions). This is for clarity and consistency, and the extended versions are referenced at various points as well as discussed in more detail under Audiences and Institutions.

How to describe the three films is also interesting in itself. We live in a post-classical era where the term 'trilogy' is as much a convenient PR term as generic description, yet **The Lord of the Rings** films are not, in essence, a trilogy (as discussed under Genre) as in their totality they form a continuous whole. However, in institutional terms for their releases, they are, appealing to the audience knowledge and understanding of the cinematic trilogy. Where the three films are referred to as

"To bear a Ring of Power is to be alone"

a trilogy it is therefore meant in cinematic terms, and it is acknowledged that Tolkien wrote the stories as one book, with them being split by his publisher. They are also referred to as a trio, a triptych, an odyssey, a series, a cycle and so on. Also, where the films are referred to as 'Jackson's' this is again for economy and it is acknowledged that the status of auteur is an interesting and problematic one (discussed under the section of the same name).

And lastly, looking at the three films has meant not only a journey of tremendous enjoyment but also of acknowledging that for everything dicussed there is far more beyond it. So in a sense this Guide is merely a starting point, and recognises that there is an enormity of filmic study to be had from the films and their remarkable creation of the diegetic world of Middle Earth and all its inhabitants.

NOTES:

A note on style

Each of the three films will generally be referred to under their individual titles or abbreviations (**The Fellowship…, The Return…**), and only as **The Lord of the Rings** when being discussed collectively.

Origins

JRR Tolkien

It is hard to imagine how an Oxford Professor's lifetime preoccupation with languages and myth has led to the global phenomenon that has become *The Lord of the Rings*, from its books to its computer games, mugs and figurines. In the run up to the release of *The Fellowship of the Ring* (2003) there was much musing and speculation in the press of what exactly John Ronald Reuel Tolkien would have made of it all. Who can know? But it would seem the literary cult of the books has translated onto film into an even larger, more expansive phenomenon that maintains the essence of the books and seeks to share it with new audiences.

Tolkein's first book, *The Hobbit*, was published in 1937, following the adventures of Bilbo Baggins. Despite his intention for *The Silmarillion* to be his next publication, it was in fact *The Lord of the Rings*, in 1954. It was the result of literally years of labour. Tolkien's well-documented obsession with languages meant that he created several of his own, which were high and low Elvish, Dwarvish and Adunaic. His belief in the power of myth and ability to create a world almost as part of our ancient history means he remains the most influential fantasy author of all time. As Peter Jackson has said: 'That's what separates it from other fantasy novels. It feels more historical rather than fantastical. You believe in the myth.'[1] But myth it is, and given the importance of the study of the signs and signification of myth and their meaning by semiotics in film and media analysis, this must be remembered.

The books were soon cult reading material, and in the hippie era the world of Middle Earth was translated into song (Led Zepellin, Marc Bolan and even Leonard Nimoy referred to it) and, as some say, to the world of computer programming language[2]. They have maintained their status as adored fiction and, despite often being denied entry to the literary canon, fans over successive generations have found the books endlessly rich in detail and fascinatingly fantastical.

It is the emphasis on authenticity that this Guide will return to again and again, the depth of the world depicting a believable space in which cultures are given their own identities, histories and myths. For years the books were considered unfilmable and it is easy to see why, with their spectacular locations, races of different sizes, imaginary beasts, not to mention a 'villain' comprised only of an eye engulfed in flame. Jackson's version of the books was not however the first. Ralph Bakshi made an animated version of *The Fellowship of the Ring* (and part of *The Two Towers*) called *JRR Tolkien's The Lord of the Rings* in 1978 (it was this that Jackson says inspired him to read the books). A follow up was never made. Then there came a BBC Radio serial of the books in 1981 (starring Ian Holm as the voice of Frodo). But still no trio of films had been attempted. Jackson and his partner Fran Walsh obtained the film rights and began the long process of adapting them, first for Miramax (who would eventually pass on the project after wanting to make the three books into one film), and ultimately for New Line. They were attempting to film not only what was considered unfilmable, but books that were much-loved and fiercely guarded by armies of loyal fans. Jackson addressed these issues in a series of canny manoeuvres as discussed under Audiences and Institutions. For now, it is enough to say that New Line's greenlighting of the project meant the three films were made concurrently, mobilising an enormous cinematic project, undeniably the most ambitious film-making exercise ever

undertaken. The audacious labour of love for Tolkien seemed in turn to have become a labour of love for Peter Jackson and an enormous cast and crew. The films have been accepted by the Tolkien fan community, and moved far wider afield. What remains of interest now is just how, and why, this happened.

NOTES:

1   Brooks, X, 'The Ring Cycle', *The Guardian*, 22 May 2004
2   *The Rough Guide to the Lord of the Rings*, London: Penguin, 2004

Broadly speaking, studying narrative means studying the way stories are told. With reference to cinema, in particular Hollywood, this means the examination of the ways film is constructed to best and most effectively tell a story and engage the audience's interest. It is interesting that Tolkien's obsession with myth, with its enduring cultural impact regardless of its nature, has been adapted into one of if not the most powerful modes of contemporary storytelling – film. Also of note is that what may to some have seemed narratively inaccessible on the page, somehow irrelevant, found vast audiences and enormous popularity on the screen. This says much about the study of *narratology* in relation to film as a universal language employing visual as well as verbal codes to appeal to a wide and diverse range of audiences.

The study of narrative, narratology, is of course not confined to film. All the way back to Vladimir Propp in the 1920s theorists have been attempting to decode the cultural and structural meaning behind storytelling. Later cultural theorists such as Saussure investigated language from a linguistic perspective, which argued that language had meaning above its words alone, formed in the connotation and further denotation of words (**connotation** being a word's literal meaning; **denotation** meaning the social meaning or associations of the word)[3]. This idea, that language had a social dimension of meaning, was then furthered by Claude Lévi-Strauss who believed this could be applied not just to words but to stories. Roland Barthes then began to look at the role of all cultural myths, from news stories to adverts (signs, as he called them), from the point of view of how they allowed socially constructed dominant ideologies (for example patriarchy) to seem so common and accepted within a culture that they are taken as natural. This forms the basis of much of the study of narrative – how it seeks to potentially maintain the hegemonic status quo.

What Tolkien would have made of such deconstructions of myth (which he believed in so fundamentally) does not take away from the fact that in creating, in a sense, a false history to his own story his use of myth was entirely constructive. That semiotics can be applied to the visual storytelling of film offers a 'way in' not just to studying narrative but mise-en-scène, costume, soundtrack and so on for their coded meaning. This section will examine *The Lord of the Rings* films from the perspectives of the principle narrative theories relating to film: those of classical Hollywood narrative and its use of time, space and cause (including a look at Propp's study of narrative patterns); Todorov's well-known analysis of the three-act structure; the depths of knowledge applied in the films and their effects upon spectorship and engagement; and finally a look at the debates around the tensions between narrative and spectacle often noted in contemporary cinema.

CLASSICAL HOLLYWOOD NARRATIVE

One of the arguments made by Russian folklorist Vladimir Propp was that no matter how diverse narratives may seem, there were and are a limited number of stories to be told. Despite its staggering amount of detail, including the invention of new languages, countless new words and of course the creation of an entirely fictional, mythical world in Middle Earth, this is applicable to *The Lord of the Rings*. The trajectory of the story is surprisingly simple. It is a **quest** narrative. A reversal of a Holy Grail mission, here the aim is to destroy the One Ring. This is the goal (cause) of the story. At a time of post-classsical Hollywood and the self-conscious styling of films, this could be seen as a throwback to traditional storytelling but with incredible new effects. The quest then is a **journey** plot (as well as a chase), and on this

The Ring's destruction drives the narrative

journey the space presented will vary and change greatly. There must also be the creation of some form of time frame, and of course there is at all times the element of cause and effect – the Ring is the cause and the driving motivator for the story. It is, ultimately, a story of good versus evil (discussed in more detail later), a universal theme of narrative.

'A narrative begins with one situation; a series of changes occurs according to a pattern of cause and effect; finally, a new situation arises that brings about the end of the narrative.'[4] *The Lord of the Rings* films abide by the rules of classical Hollywood narrative storytelling. In this they demonstrate clear **time frames**, **space** and **causality**, with events following a linear, chronological trajectory (although with some manipulation of time in the use of flashback, etc.). Classical Hollywood narrative contains conventions that are so ingrained in viewers that the structure itself seems 'natural' rather than artificially constructed. How narrative works in presenting story information within the mind of the spectator calls into question the very nature of film-watching. All filmic elements, within classical Hollywood storytelling, work together to best tell the story. The **diegesis** (story world) is of the utmost importance and all filmic elements, including costumes, settings and the use of continuity editing are all used to ensure the story is told as 'invisibly' as possible. Classical Hollywood is generally associated with a clear cause-and-effect structure, with **characters** acting as the main agents of both cause and audience identification. It abides by Todorov's three-act structure, which is here analysed in relation to *The Lord of the Rings* films.

NOTES:

3. Storey, John, *An Introductory Guide to Cultural Theory and Popular Culture*, 1993
4. Bordwell and Thompson, *Film Art: An Introduction*, 1997, p90

Narrative

The story of **The Lord of the Rings** overall is linear. However while it can be seen as a simple quest narrative, filmically the action regularly switches from situation to situation, character to character, space to space, telling of simultaneous events in different locations and at times altering their temporal order. The editing together of these multiple plots and storylines is vital in creating and maintaining coherence (and this is one of the most remarkable achievements of the films). In fact, recalling each film, it is surprisingly easy to recount the events and overall storylines presented, but much more difficult to remember in exactly what *sequence* they were presented. Added to this is the fact that while this one story is told across three films, each film must also abide by certain narrative conventions to satisfy as a stand-alone film in its own right.

The narrative is fractured – we follow not one group, but several as the story progresses. In **The Fellowship...** we first follow the hobbits, joined by Aragorn, and edited in parallel are the actions of Saruman and the plight of Gandalf. There then follows the formation of the Fellowship, who we follow as one entity in their journey juxtaposed against the plottings of Saruman. But as the Fellowship breaks at the end of the film, come **The Two Towers** we are following several smaller groups – Frodo and Sam, as they attempt to reach Mordor, Aragorn, Legolas and Gimli as they search for Merry and Pippin, and find Gandalf. All three groups encounter new characters – Sam and Frodo meet Gollum; Aragorn, etc. encounter the court of Rohan, introducing Théoden, Éowyn and Éomer among others; and Merry and Pippin meet Treebeard. These are not incidental characters (there *are* no incidental characters in the films, everyone has a narrative purpose, even the extras in creating credible worlds), even if their purpose may not be clear from the outset (the narrative necessity of Treebeard and the Ents is not shown until towards the end of **The Two Towers** when they destroy Isengard in a parallel storyline to Saruman's defeat at Helm's Deep). Tied to the presentation and development of these storylines is the importance of editing (which is analysed later in Film Language). To fully understand the narrative structure of the films they must be looked at first in relation to the primary elements of classical Hollyood narrative, and also examined from the perspective of prominent theories of narration and spectatorship.

Space

As indicated the three most basic elements to classical Hollywood storytelling are how the story is presented in time, space and causality. All film action takes place within space and time, and with classical Hollywood narration the two will be heavily linked to cause and effect, which predominantly stems from character.

In terms of space, the numerous locations featured in **The Lord of the Rings**, while continually allowing for the story to move forward as it must (the locations are all intricately linked to the narrative as well as offering visual stimulation to the viewer), might seem bewildering to audiences were they not firmly established within an over-arching geography. This geographical space is Middle Earth, established first by the maps and the voice over used in the opening prologue of the first film. This space is given its own history by the detail of the story therefore adding much to its authenticity. Also important here is the use of **displacement** – the world being presented is not our own, the use of distant settings allowing for the exploration of both universal and contemporaneous themes at a safe distance.

Despite perhaps not knowing exactly where the characters are going, the space within the film is presented as coherent. With Sam and Frodo in particular, we know what their destination is – Mordor – and therefore their quest is a physical journey that traverses multiple locations but with one sole purpose. This is linked to cause and effect by being the only place where the Ring can be destroyed, which reinforces an internal logic. The journeys of the other characters are still mapped according to space, with their varying quests (rescuing Pippin and Merry, aiding Rohan or Gondor) leading them forwards. In this way space actually works to keep the narrative continuously driving forward and it is notable that very few locations are visited more than once, apart from the film's haven, The Shire (discussed in more detail under Locations/Setting). The arc of the story relating to a physical drive through terrain being mapped by its relation to Mordor creates a coherent forward-moving space without the use of non-diegetic intertitles (used only at the beginning of **The Fellowship...** upon the introduction of Frodo). There may be brief moments of respite identified through various spaces (such as Lothlórien and Rivendell) but they are transitory and still form part of the narrative's overall relentless motion forward. There are only a few instances where space moves inexplicably, often connoting a mental/spiritual connection between characters; for instance the distance between Arwen and Aragon is bridged by 'dreams', and in the films' most dramatic change of space, Frodo, alone in Shelob's lair, is suddenly in woodland, being offered a helping hand (literally) by the elf, Galadriel.

Time

Temporally, modern audiences are highly accustomed to seeing films that present story events out of chronological order, subconsciously filtering and ordering events and information. But all events within a film must happen in time, whether it is compressed time in the form of montage, or flashback, flashforward, or even just how scenes are

NOTES:

edited to allow for screen time to be used most effectively in presenting relevant information and omitting or curtailing that which is of less pertinence. These techniques should benefit the presentation and understanding of the film's plot, and the viewer can filter and order this information. Time, within the three films, involves space – the timeframe is of an ancient world, described as the Third Age of Middle Earth. So we are looking at a past. The diegesis does also incorporate the future, through seeing stones and mirrors or visions; however in keeping with the thematic concerns of the story these futures are only possibilities. Time, in this sense, is only certain if it is the past or the present.

We have no preface as there is in *Star Wars* – 'A long time ago in a galaxy far far away…' – but we do have a prologue that provides large amounts of background information very quickly. While the overall appearance of time in the narrative is coherent, filmically time is regularly manipulated and compressed where appropriate.

'A film does not just start, it begins'[5]. The use of time and space in establishing the story world in a film's opening minutes is vital, and often involves the manipulation of time. Each film of the series begins with a prologue that uses time in a non-linear way and for a different purpose:

1 *The Fellowship of the Ring* prologue – Establishes Middle Earth (space), history (time), Sauron and the power of the Ring (cause).

2 *The Two Towers* prologue – Shows Gandalf's journey with the Balrog from *The Fellowship of the Ring* (flashback), but showing more, and hinting that Gandalf is not dead, but before we know it is cut short. It is implied to be Frodo's dream.

3 *The Return of the King* prologue – The corruption and deterioration of Sméagol to Gollum on finding the Ring over a long period of time (presented in flashback).

Each prologue offers narrative information (as well as spectacle, as discussed later), but for different ends (their length also differs). **The Fellowship…** prologue also serves as a prologue for all three films.

This opening of the entire saga tells the backstory of the Ring and of Middle Earth. We are introduced to the history behind the One Ring. The information being presented is actually from Tolkien's *The Silmarillion* (which he wrote prior to *The Lord of the Rings* but which was not published until afterwards). It contains certain key characteristics of the ways in which film can compress and manipulate story time through screen duration. Firstly, it has a **narrator**. This is a character narrator (a homodiegetic narrator), Galadriel, and it is also notably the voice of one of the film's few then widely-known stars, Cate Blanchett. She begins in a different language, early on establishing thematic elements of the story – she talks of the earth, of the water, and of course, of history (this prologue will cover vast periods of diegetic time). This opening sequence tells of the origin of the Ring, i.e. how it came to be; and it establishes space (by its use of locations), time (by showing characters in 'ancient' costumes) and effect (the power of the Ring). It also shows cause – the principal evil character, Sauron (shown for the first and only time, other than in similar flashbacks, in semi-human form), here spectacularly destroyed, with the Ring passing to Gollum and then Bilbo. So this sequence provides a large amount of information with great economy and speed, moving through time and space very quickly, using the unifying technique of the voice over to make sense of the information. This opening also offers the audience an immediate 'spectacle' in the battle (examined in further detail later in this chapter).

The opening to *The Two Towers* uses time in a different way. It is simultaneously a flashback

Sauron and the Ring establish cause

and a flashforward. We witness a brief retelling of Gandalf's fight against the Balrog in the Mines of Moria (it is of note that the second film offers no précis of the first film for viewers who may not have seen it). We are watching action we have seen previously, in **The Fellowship…**. This time, however, as Gandalf falls we follow him, not the other characters, as he plunges downwards with great speed and, again, visual spectacle. Again the audience is provided with a sequence of effects-driven drama. It also implies there was and is more to tell about Gandalf, and while it flashes back to the previous film, it also flashes forward, by casting doubt that Gandalf is actually dead. The sequence is interrupted (Frodo wakes, implying it was a dream) but is completed later, as Gandalf himself recounts the remainder of the story (as a flashback to this fragmented flashback, as it were) on meeting with Aragorn, Legolas and Gimli.

In **The Return…**, we are not at first given any idea of the time frame for the action of the prologue, but upon hearing his voice we become aware that the character we are watching is Gollum, prior to his degeneration. As well as providing character knowledge (and reaffirming just how powerful the Ring is for Gollum, following on from his would-be betrayal shown at the end of the previous film), it also compresses time. In a truly horrific sequence we see Sméagol becoming Gollum over what we must assume is a long period. The changes in his appearance cleverly

---

NOTES:

5. ibid., p99

Narrative

Sméagol's transformation

illustrate the passing of time, and bring us up to date more or less to the current character. This sequence provides a backstory to Gollum, who by the end of the second film we know is to play a key and dastardly role in the fate of Frodo and the Ring. It not only enhances our knowledge of Gollum but also his prior similarities to Frodo, and acts as a cautionary tale of the fate that may await him if Frodo cannot destroy the Ring. By showing this parallel, the tension is heightened.

On top of these tightly constructed flashbacks there are shorter uses of flashbacks in the three films. These refresh information for the viewers – in *The Return...*, brief flashbacks are used, all to accompany the talk of previous events. There is a short sequence showing Boromir's death, another showing Frodo being stabbed by a Black Rider on Weathertop, both events from the first film (perhaps a reminder to audiences who may not have seen the film since its release two years prior?). In keeping with the themes of the story, any use of flashforward (showing something from the future) is only showing what 'might' be (when Frodo looks into the mirror of Galadriel, for example). There are no hints as to the outcome, and this is vital to maintain tension as the story moves towards both its smaller climactic moments (such as the falling of Gandalf, or defeat of the Urak Hai at Helm's Deep) and also its ultimate conclusion.

As the story nears its climax, the time frame becomes more and more specific and more akin to 'real time'. Considered at greater length under Use of Camera and Editing, the presentation of 'parallel action' and storylines becomes more urgent. In the case of *The Lord of the Rings*, this is demonstrated best by the conclusion – as Frodo and Sam try desperately to reach the top of Mount Doom (only to be confronted by Gollum), simultaneously Aragorn and his army are about to be overwhelmed by the armies of Mordor. The time line for both and the parallels of the situations heighten the tension in both plot lines, which are of course linked by the one unifying goal – the defeat of Sauron. So the narrative of *The Lord of the Rings*, whilst being relatively simple in its plot, is fractured. We follow parallel action of different characters in difference spaces, but through careful editing are persuaded that events are all happening at the same time. This creates coherence, but the unifying factor to all the action and its multiple interwoven storylines is **cause**.

Cause

The third and most important element of classical Hollywood narrative, causality is for the most part created by characters. It is what drives a narrative forward. The causal motivation for the entire story is the destruction of the Ring, and the defeat of Sauron in order to save Middle Earth. This cause is the same for all the 'good' characters, even if their parts to play are different. The fight of men against Saruman and Sauron's armies are still connected to this one over-arching goal, which allows for the narrative to remain clear at all times for the viewer, with all such plights also acting as obstacles to raise tension in the overall narrative drive. For all the film's spectacular battles, the less visible, seductive power of the Ring as it gradually begins to drive Frodo mad is continually kept paramount, as, therefore, is the danger of the whole quest, in the forefront of the viewer's minds.

In keeping with the themes of the story the characters can very much be divided into good and evil characters. There are vast numbers of characters in *The Lord of the Rings*, and as mentioned while some may seem incidental they rarely if ever actually are (the removal of a less pivotal character from the book such as Tom Bombadil from the film adaptations may have upset some fans of the book but such 'streamlining' of the story world effectively sacrifices all the extraneous strands to maintain a tight narrative). There is room for characters to oscillate between both good and evil (for example Boromir, Faramir, and particularly Frodo and Gollum) but as a general rule there is a clear boundary between the two.

As Tolkien was interested in the power of myth, Russian folklorist Vladimir Propp was interested in attempting to prove that narratives, regardless of form or cultural origin, all had structural similarities that could be identified. He identified seven **character functions** which he called 'spheres of action'.[6] His theory, which was written in 1927 but not translated into English until the 1960s[7], related to Russian folktales but was, upon translation, seen as a useful method for analysing the universal characteristics of story inherent in classical Hollywood storytelling. More than one function could be held by one character, but the functions remained constant. As shown, they relate to these ideas of 'good' and 'bad' characters. They are:

- The villain
- The donor
- The helper
- The princess (and her father)
- The dispatcher
- The hero
- The false hero.

If applied to *The Lord of the Rings* these character functions could look like this –

NOTES:

6. Turner, *Film as Social Practice*, 1988, p71
7. ibid.
8. ibid., p69

- **The villain**
  Sauron, Saruman

- **The donor**
  Bilbo, Galadriel

- **The helper**
  Sam, Aragorn, Legolas, Gimli, Pippin, Merry, Boromir, Éomer, Faramir, etc.

- **The princess**
  Arwen (and her father, Elrond), Éowyn (and father figure, Théoden)

- **The dispatcher**
  Gandalf

- **The hero**
  Frodo

- **The false hero**
  Gollum.

Around this limited number of spheres of action are a maximum of 31 narrative functions broadly dividing into **Preparation**, **Complication**, **Transference**, **Struggle**, **Return** and **Recognition**.[8] This demonstrates that the character functions within the story are clearly defined, but due to the complexity of the story there may be many characters performing the same 'sphere of action'. For instance there are multiple helpers, and multiple villains (Sauron may be the 'true' villain but around him are others, from Saruman to the Black Riders, Urak Hai, Orcs, the Balrog, Wormtongue, Gollum, Shelob, not to mention the numerous other creatures with malevolent intentions). Also in terms of the narrative functions identified by Propp, one of the resolving spheres of action is the marriage of the hero to the princess (this romantic 'dual plotting' is also a key feature of classical Hollywood narrative). This calls into question exactly who the hero of this story actually is. Both Aragorn and Sam are rewarded with marriage, and both demonstrate heroic characteristics (it could be argued that Sam ultimately is the hero of the story). Frodo, on the other hand, is the lone Ring bearer and therefore in many ways the central hero, but

he is not rewarded in this way. He also ultimately refuses to destroy the Ring and is aided by the false hero, Gollum, and although this is glossed over to some extent in the subsequent praise and triumph of the hobbits, it could be argued that Frodo is saved from becoming the false hero by Gollum. Simply, Gollum's hunger for the Ring is the greater and more violent of the two, but nevertheless Frodo's capacity to become this false hero is realised and then averted.

A Proppian analysis therefore demonstrates that despite the length and complexities of **The Lord of the Rings**, its structure is very similar to those of traditional narrative and can be broken down into its specific elements. Character traits and motivations are vital to cause and to the narrative. In **The Lord of the Rings** these are kept fairly simple and interrelated, with the two opposing forces of good and evil acting as contrasting reference points. As stated, many, if not all, of the principal characters have the same causal motivation – to destroy the Ring and defeat Sauron. This established goal informs all that follows. However around these principals are multiple characters with the same functions demonstrating that these character types are just that and while they can be structurally useful will not necessarily serve as anything other than agents of cause.

Another function of character as cause is the combination of the personal journey with the narrative one. For example, as a self-exiled heir, Aragorn's conflicts over his role as King must be overcome in order for him to rule, and this he does, providing Middle Earth with a leader after Sauron's destruction, therefore restoring a new equilibrium. This is after he has led battles and summoned the dead army that only he could, as heir. Other members of the Fellowship such as Gimli, Legolas and even Gandalf, are there purely to see the task completed and the evil overcome, therefore their character motivations are clear. Which is not to say they have no character

development, as with Merry and Pippin, but it is more in line with personal developments (e.g. the friendship between Legolas and Gimli, the maturing of Pippin and Merry). One critic stated that '**LOTR** is not about a narrative arc or the growth of the characters, but about a long series of episodes in which the essential nature of the characters is demonstrated again and again'.[9] To some extent this is true, but it discounts much of the development of particularly Frodo and Sam, and of course the drastically oscillating character of Gollum.

What this type of analysis fails to account for is the role character traits have in fostering audience **identification**. Emotional involvement and focalisation is essential in order to maintain the interest and involvement of the spectator. This area of characterisation relates far more to issues of **spectatorship** and **representation**, (discussed in greater detail in Representation). For now it must be acknowledged that while the character functions within the films can be easily assigned to the Proppian model, the further dimension of involvement so vital to films is not highlighted by this method of analysis. While it may deal well with cause and its importance to narrative, it is entirely text-focused and omits not only the important ways in which audiences construct narratives by their cognitive processes, but how cultural ideologies are inherent in the representation of areas such as gender and race (for instance the patriarchal affirmation of the hero marrying the princess). Taking that as an area to be discussed, we now turn to another, complimentary form of theoretical narrative structure and analysis that again relates to Hollywood storytelling, the **three-act structure**.

NOTES:

9. Roger Ebert quoted in *The Rough Guide to The Lord of the Rings*, 2004, p151

Narrative

TODOROV AND THE THREE-ACT STRUCTURE

Tzvetan Todorov identified a three-act structure to narrative. The first is **equilibrium**, where everything seems stable. Due to events in the story, this is disrupted to form a state of **disequilibrium**, and the third part of a **new equilibrium** can only be reached when the disequilibrium is confronted and defeated. Something must have altered from the first to the final equilibrium, hence the first is often called a **false equilibrium** – if everything really was stable and normal, no disequilibrium would follow. This three-act structure is another feature of classical Hollywood narrative.

So how could this apply to *The Lord of the Rings*? If looking at a three-act structure, arguably the story is already divided into three separate acts, with *The Fellowship...* as Act One, *The Two Towers* as Act Two, and so on. Looking at the whole over-arching story in relation to Todorov there is also a three-act structure regardless of the three separate films – the **false equilibrium** at the opening is the party and life in the Shire with the Ring seemingly dormant. The **disequilibrium** begins when Gandalf realises what the Ring is and dispatches Frodo to leave the Shire. From then on there is continuous disequilibrium. Even moments of seeming victory and therefore new equilibrium, such as the defeat of Saruman's army at Helm's Deep, are transitory. **Equilibrium** cannot be fully restored until the Ring (and Sauron) is destroyed.

With *The Fellowship...*, although we have a brief equilibrium at the opening, as Frodo and Bilbo live peacefully within the idyllic Shire and prepare for a party, we, the audience, already know that Bilbo's is the One Ring following the prologue, and we therefore know this to be a false equilibrium (we also thus

know more than the character within the diegesis, see Hierarchies of Knowledge). Once Frodo is dispatched from the Shire the story is in a state of more or less constant disequilibrium until the Ring is destroyed at the end of the third film, at which point we have a new equilibrium, with evil destroyed. So even given its length, multiple characters and storylines, *The Lord of the Rings* abides by this structure overall. The dominant act is that of disequilibrium, inevitable given the length of the story on the screen – but what complicates this is how the individual films must also function according to these rules.

Due to the story being shot as three films, the usual expectations of cinema audiences are disrupted. Both *The Fellowship...* and *The Two Towers* end with a state of disequilibrium (which is of a more urgent nature in the second film). Each must stand alone enough as an individual film with its own story to fulfill viewing pleasure, but must also fit into a larger whole and work in an anticipatory way for the following film. (That these films are not 'sequels' but an entire story renders them the most prominent cinema trilogy since *Star Wars*, with *The Matrix* trilogy (1999-2003) failing to live up to audience expectation. *The Lord of the Rings* is narratively far more coherent than the other two franchises.) So there must be some forms of resolution, yet also the opening up of storylines. How is the three-act structure manifested in each film?

The Fellowship of the Ring

Act One

Frodo and Sam leave the Shire, encounter Pippin and Merry, are led by Aragorn, and Frodo is injured by the Black Riders; Arwen takes Frodo to Rivendell, defeating the Black Riders at the river.

Act Two

Rivendell; the forming of the Fellowship, their departure and journey, the Mines of Moria and Gandalf's 'death'.

Act Three

Arrival at Lothlórien; Saruman's Urak Hai track the Fellowship; Boromir attempts to take the Ring; the attack from the Urak Hai, the capture of Pippin and Merry, the death of Boromir, and the escape of Frodo and Sam.

The Two Towers

Act One

Frodo and Sam are lost; Aragorn, Legolas and Gimli search for Pippin and Merry, who escape and meet Treebeard; Rohan is introduced, Aragorn *et al* encounter Gandalf.

Act Two

The arrival at Rohan; Gollum persuades Sam and Frodo to enter Mordor a different way, they are captured; Théoden et al flee to Helm's Deep, Aragorn's fall and recovery; Arwen leaves Rivendell.

Act Three

The Battle of Helm's Deep; the destruction of Isengard; the release of Frodo, Sam and Gollum and the impending betrayal by Gollum.

The Return of the King

Act One

Frodo, Sam and Gollum continue towards Mordor, Pippin looks into the seeing stone and he and Gandalf ride to Minas Tirith to

NOTES:

warn of attack; Sam discovers Gollum's treachery, Arwen refuses to leave Middle Earth and Elrond reforges the sword of Isildur; Frodo, Sam and Gollum begin the climb into Mordor and Sauron's army is dispatched; Pippin lights the beacons of Gondor.

Act Two

Rohan rides to Gondor, Elrond visits Aragorn, Minas Tirith is attacked, Faramir is saved; the Battle of Pelennor Fields; Aragorn commands the Dead Army, Frodo sends Sam away and is lured into the tunnel by Gollum. He is attacked and stung by giant spider Shelob, the battle is won, Éowyn slays the Witch King, Théoden dies, Sam slays Shelob and rescues Frodo; they begin to cross Mordor in disguise.

Act Three

Frodo and Sam's final ascent to Mount Doom, the massing of Aragorn's army outside Mordor, the destruction of the Ring and Sauron; Aragorn is crowned King of Gondor and is reunited with Arwen, the hobbits return to the Shire. Sam marries, Bilbo; Gandalf and Frodo leave across the sea, Sam returns to his family.

These are approximations, and are particularly difficult in relation to the final film, where in a sense there are *four* acts, or three and a long epilogue. But broadly speaking each film abides by the three-act structure of Hollywood narrative but the first two films do not end with a new equilibrium but with degrees of disequilibrium. The defeat of the Urak Hai at the end of **The Fellowship...** and their failure to capture Frodo is in one sense a satisfying outcome; however Aragorn, Legolas and Gimli set off to track a captured Merry and Pippin, with Sam and Frodo starting their trek towards Mordor. It is harder to delineate the different acts in the latter two films as there are multiple storylines occurring simultaneously. For instance in **The Two Towers**, the defeat of Saruman at both Helm's Deep and Isengard offers some satisfying resolution. But this is then undercut by the anticipated betrayal by Gollum. They are

commercial films and thus must abide by certain audience expectations and still have beginnings, middles and ends, and therefore some form of narrative resolution. But the first two films cannot resolve the narrative overall and must also create anticipation for the final chapter. Contemporary audiences are adept at understanding the concept of the filmic trio. The very fact that each film's title follows the overall title of **The Lord of the Rings** and that from the start there has been an awareness that the story comes in three parts, signalling a shift away from standard resolution patterns, can be seen as allowing for a deviation of narrative norms, while still adhering to the overall three-act structure.

As mentioned, the final instalment, **The Return of the King**, in addition to a three-act structure, contains an epilogue. After the destruction of Sauron and the Ring and the crowning of Aragorn as King, the hobbits return to the Shire, Sam marries (a standard narrative resolution for the hero) and Frodo leaves Middle Earth. While this may problematise a three-act structure for that particular film, when seeing the three films as a continuous narrative it is necessary to tie up the fates of the major characters. In the same way that narrative false equilibrium lasts for some time in the first film, the new equilibrium should arguably at least equal it in the final film to balance the story.

HIERARCHIES OF KNOWLEDGE

The amount of information given to audiences, in relation to the amount of knowledge held by characters within a film, greatly affects the spectator's response. For example if we know no more than a particular character, we will experience **surprise**, but if we know more, we will experience **suspense**. A combination of both is often employed in classical Hollywood narrative to create interest.

These methods are called **restricted** and **omniscient** or **unrestricted** narration.

The Lord of the Rings films move between the opposite sides of the depth of knowledge – restricted and omniscient or unrestricted narration – employing both. This is the **hierarchy of knowledge**.[10] At times we the viewer know what the characters do, at times less, at times more, and these will all create different effects on the viewer and the story. Restricted narration is when information is deliberately kept hidden from either us the audience or particular characters within the diegetic world. Unrestricted is when all information is presented, and this is unlikely to exist until the end of a film, because if it were, we would lose interest in finding out what may happen.

Although it may seem when watching a film such as **The Lord of the Rings** that we are witnessing events as they unfold within the diegetic world of Middle Earth, as with all films there is a complex dynamic of the flow of information between the audience, the characters and the plot.

In terms of the hierarchy of knowledge, the films start off with the viewer higher up than any of the characters because we know what Bilbo and even Gandalf do not – that he is in possession of the One Ring. As the narrative progresses we then start to learn things alongside the characters; for example that Saruman serves Sauron we learn only when Gandalf does (hence surprise), or when Frodo discovers that Strider/Aragorn will not harm but help him. But we know less than some characters, as we are surprised to learn, alongside Frodo, that Aragorn is in fact a king in disguise. The flux of information the viewer is allowed access to in relation to the characters creates a combination of both surprise and suspense.

Moments in the films when we know only what the characters know – to create

---

NOTES:

10. Bordwell and Thompson, *Film Art: An Introduction*, 1997, p103

anticipation and surprise – are many, perhaps one of the most prominent being when Frodo is led into Shelob's lair in **The Return...**, not knowing, like us, what awaits him: 'Restricted narration tends to create greater curiosity and surprise for the viewer'.[11] Similarly at Helm's Deep and the battle of Pelennor Fields we cannot know any more than the main characters in order for us to endure the tension (aided by audience identification). At Helm's Deep, when Aragorn identifies the torch-carrying Urak Hai as potentially disastrous, we the audience know why, having been shown Saruman's discovery of gun powder and the Deep's 'weakness', whereas Aragorn acts on instinct, thus coding him once more as valuable leader and our point of identification. This minor fluctuation of audience knowledge is another example of the complexities of both audience identification but also, vitally, participation (we hope as he does that the Urak Hai will be stopped).

Perhaps the use of unrestricted narration for the audience is most pivotal at the end of **The Two Towers** and through **The Return...** when we know what Sam and Frodo do not – that Gollum will betray them. This heightens our sense of suspense. Such use of restricted and unrestricted/omniscient information in this way has a bearing on the objectivity or subjectivity of the viewer. While objective narration offers us access to characters (and therefore plot points) via their external performance (external focalisation), subjectivity creates a depth of knowledge where we can see/experience events from a particular character's point of view (internal focalisation). The films use point of view shots at various times (discussed in Use of Camera) but it is in the depiction of Gollum that we experience subjectivity in order to allow us knowledge no other character has.

Gollum's split personality and his conversations with himself cleverly allow him within the diegetic world to be in essence talking to himself. What he, eventually, reveals

is that Sméagol has overcome Gollum – he plans to kill Sam and Frodo in order to take the Ring. This knowledge informs the climax of **The Two Towers**, as Frodo and Sam (now trusting of Gollum) follow him unawares, while we the audience know differently. It is a narrative device stretching from literature to film and even to pantomime (where the audience delights in shouting 'he's behind you' to a deliberately oblivious stage character). These straight-to-audience sequences also offer us explanations for his character's erratic behaviour – without the articulation of these inner monologues, we would have no access to Gollum's schizophrenic battle, and his behaviour would not make sense. As Sam also discovers this, we ally ourselves with him, seeing more objectively Frodo's increasingly subjective, blinded trust in Gollum as entirely misguided. However once Sam has had his suspicions confirmed (upon discovering the discarded Lembas bread) and Frodo himself has learned of Gollum's treachery, the hierarchy of knowledge has levelled and we are able to anticipate and dread the contents of the tunnel alongside Frodo, knowing little more than him aside from Gollum's plotting. It also situates Sam more and more as the audience's point of identification, culminating in his horror as Frodo refuses to throw the Ring into Mount Doom. He, like us, is not under the influence of the Ring – unlike both Frodo and Gollum.

This is another area where the audience sees more than many of the other characters. For example, when Frodo puts on the Ring during the attack on Weathertop, he is invisible to his friends, but is in fact more visible to the Black Riders who are suddenly transformed in this other dimension to show the white, ghostly faces of Kings, in total contrast to their usual dark facelessness. We, the audience, also witness this alternate state of reality. Frodo, and the audience, are allowed access to a level of consciousness/reality denied to the other characters. This initially allies us with Frodo but gradually that identification is eroded

until finally when he places the Ring on his finger inside Mount Doom we 'see' only his absence (in other words his invisibility as the characters in the film would experience it), with the sequence framed for us from Sam's, not Frodo's, point of view, as objective witness to the events.

The possession of knowledge within the story world also varies between other characters, with some implied to be wise (such as Gandalf and Galadriel) by knowing much of what is going to happen; and others knowing very little (characters such as Pippin, Merry and initially Sam, who perhaps more than any other character evolves to become the audience's main point of identification). Ultimately as we near the end of the story, none of the characters, nor the audience, has any different level of knowledge, it is all restricted. The climax of the story must elevate the viewers. With this story, the desired outcome is obvious throughout the three films, but as with most narratives it is *how* this is achieved, and the tension of whether they will succeed, that provides the viewer with an incentive to keep watching. Abiding by the classical Hollywood narrative pattern of resolution, audiences expect a satisfactory ending. At this point, on one hand the audience know no more than each set of characters, but we are witness to the possible failure and disaster of both storylines (the failure of Frodo to destroy the Ring and the imminent destruction of Aragorn and the army outside). As Frodo and Gollum seemingly tumble off the edge of the precipice, we know no more than Sam and he is again our point of identification. However once the Ring lies on the lava in Mount Doom, the audience alone is witness to the close up melting and destruction of the Ring. We enjoy the gratification of watching the characters as they realise what has happened, but share their concern as, like them, we do not know what may happen now to Frodo and Sam.

The Epilogue of **The Return...**, with its final

NOTES:

11. ibid, p104

restoration of equilibrium, offers us Aragorn as King, and both he and Sam married, but with a final journey element for Bilbo, Gandalf and Frodo. There is one final hierarchy of knowledge in which we are aligned with the hobbits, as Frodo departs with Bilbo and Gandalf. Neither they nor we the audience know exactly where they are bound, and as a resolution it offers the final disbanding of the Fellowship, signifying the end of the quest, and a final evenness of knowledge and information to accompany the final equilibrium.

A final journey

NARRATIVE AND SPECTACLE

As discussed further in Genre, **The Lord of the Rings** films adhere to many of the conventions of the contemporary blockbuster, a phenomenon not usually associated with narrative complexity, instead seen to focus on visual excess. All three **Lord of the Rings** films are spectacular. Many critics have derided this use of spectacle within blockbusters as a 'source of distraction and interruption'.[12] This stance assumes that classical Hollywood narrative has suffered at the hands of big-screen special effects. Such viewpoints interpret the role of narrative as being almost the main characteristic of film; yet while it is of vital importance it also interacts with a range of equally vital filmic elements. **The Lord of the Rings** films, exemplified by the prologue to **The Fellowship...**, successfully *combine* spectacle with narrative coherence – the spectacular sequences (of which there are many) form part of the overall narrative drive, so are integrated within the story, yet have

visual appeal in their own right for the spectator. The role of the spectator raises issues of audience response and the very nature of the cinema-going experience as multifaceted. 'Spectacle' does not just mean explosive effects sequences; it can also mean elements of mise-en-scène (which are fundamentally linked to narrative) and the presence of stars. As considered in Audiences and Institutions, **The Lord of the Rings** films, while featuring a few 'names', sidestep the narrative disruption caused by star presence by having lesser-known actors play the leads. Despite becoming more well known over the period of the three films' release, they would still be seen in reference to their particular character, potentially enhancing rather than disrupting narrative coherence, but utilising the increased power of the star as emphasising the power of the characters, thus having an impact on the spectator's investment in the story. Also, as considered in Representation, alongside star as spectacle is the element of desire. Several of the characters are arguably presented as objects of both the male and female gaze. This is also a form of spectacle with its own extra-diegetic pleasures for the audience.

The journey narrative of the story allows for much emphasis to be placed on the mise-en-scène, in particular the presentation of space and locations which are grandiose and vast in size, shot in ways that are highly cinematic and spectacular, but are still intrinsically linked to the narrative. The awe-inspiring views of Middle Earth are highly pleasurable and as with many of the presentations of such moments utilise CGI effects, yet do not foreground their artifice but integrate them into the presentation of the diegetic world.

It would seem that one of the films' most interesting successes is its juxtaposing of elements that are often described as opposing yet here are aligned. While spectacle is successfully linked to narrative, it does point to an interesting paradox in post-classical cinema. As the films, particularly **The Two**

Towers and **The Return...**, begin the build-up to the main battle sequences, there is a sense of dread in the audience because we know what horror is to come in the diegesis. As spectactors, however, this is matched by the excitement and anticipation of a big-screen action sequence. It does not seem superfluous or tenuous, as the argument around weakened narrative at the expense of spectacle would have it, yet we still relish the idea of a breathtaking, exhilarating screen 'experience'. As films they acknowledge both as elements of contemporary cinema – the 'intimacy' of story, and the 'thrill ride' of the blockbuster.

The spectacular presentation of action sequences revolves for the most part around **combat**. There are numerous fight sequences throughout the three films of varying degrees of size, scale and length, and these abide by the codes of action cinema, meaning they can stand alone as sequences of enjoyment for the audience, but they do still have narrative relevance. The battle of Helm's Deep is approximately 30 minutes in length and the battle for Pelennor Fields is 20 minutes long. However, these spectacular sequences, that could be argued 'suspend' narrative drive, do no such thing, in that they have narrative relevance and are juxtaposed with cuts to other lines of action (such as Frodo, Sam and Gollum). This again calls into question the assumption that spectacle and narrative are opposing forces (as well as failing to account for the fact that all films are to some extent 'spectacle') or that they are in some way problematic. Beyond this is the concept that as well as narrative codes there are levels of audience expectation for blockbuster/action cinema. *Some* degree of spectacle is expected. However a further criticism levelled at the post-classical emphasis on spectacle is the relentless drive demonstrated by some blockbusters in their narrative: 'The generation of spectacular impact within what might be described as an incessant, forward-driving narrative-spectacle context is characteristic of many recent Hollywood

NOTES:

12. King, G, *New Hollywood Cinema*, 2003, p179

Narrative

blockbusters'.[13] This could be argued in relation to **The Lord of the Rings** films, but how useful is such a statement of analysis of the impact of spectacle on narrative and vice versa? One characteristic of Jackson's films is the integration of both action/spectacle *and* narrative.

So it can be argued that the films incorporate elements of both spectacle and narrative in symbiotic ways, or that they utilise a thrusting narrative to *ensure* continuity. The film has many such action set-pieces, sequences of spectacle involving combat as autonomous scenes. Each sequence involves a distinct 'build up' to give the audience an expectation of what is to follow. Across the three films their size and impact escalates, and if looking to identify the set-pieces in each film they might look something like this:

The Fellowship of the Ring

- Prologue

- Weathertop (the fight against the Black Riders)

- The Mines of Moria

- Fight against the Urak Hai.

The Two Towers

- Prologue

- The slaying of the Urak Hai

- The attack on the way to Helm's Deep

- The battle at Helm's Deep

- The destruction of Isengard.

The Return of the King

- The siege of Osgiliath

- The battle of Pelennor Fields

- The destruction of Sauron and Mordor.

In the first prologue the enormity of the battle scene is spectacular. However, narratively it also works to demonstrate the magnitude of the power of both Sauron and the Ring. This will be the motivation (the cause) of the entire story.

While the battle sequences and large-scale attacks in the second and third films involve the fight against Saruman (Sauron's servant) and Sauron's armies, the other main plot element is the threats to both Frodo and Sam, both internally (as Frodo gradually succumbs to the allure of the Ring), and externally (through Gollum, Faramir, and various creatures including Black Riders). All the principal characters are undertaking journeys of some form, and the constant threat to them is the common theme. Action is therefore regularly balanced by character development. Throughout, spectacle is an essential component of the narrative drive, a *complimentary* rather than a competing force, in allowing the physical rendering of unreal elements to enhance, rather than diminish, the power of the diegesis.

NOTES:

13. Stringer, J, *Movie Blockbusters*, 2003, p123

WHAT IS GENRE THEORY?

Genre theory permeates the majority of contemporary Film Studies, after becoming the more popular method of analysis in the 1960s and 70s. Genre theory categorises films according to their internal patterns and external reception in order to analyse their similar visual, narrative and structural codes. It offered a move away from auteur theory – with its artistic implications – towards the study of film as not only a cultural form but as an institutional practice. Genre can be described as 'systems of orientations, expectations and conventions that circulate between industry, text and subject'.[14] If auteur and traditional narrative theory omit the audience and the industrial nature of film, genre theory allows for spectatorship to form a large part of the equation.

It is far easier to allocate films to a specific genre (set in space = science fiction; teens being killed one by one by a lone male killer = slasher/horror) than to explain the actual meaning of genre. Many writings on the subject have located it as fluid, as ever-evolving and therefore extremely hard to define. In its first instances genre was approached from three main critical perspectives – André Bazin's examination of the myth held within genres; Robert Warshow's interest in the ideological use of genre to erase contradictions within society; and Lawrence Alloway, whose work identified the importance of genre for the spectator's experience[15].

Instead of formal, stylistic characteristics offering coherent groups of films for study, André Bazin believed that the power of genre was ideological, with it being popular for its 'sympathetic material for reworking older and more universal themes'.[16] When writing about the Western, one of the most historically studied film genres, his interest lay in how its 'signs' (setting, props and so on) were 'simply signs or symbols of its profound reality, namely its myth'.[17]

This in effect removes, for example, the Western from being purely about an American experience and renders it more universal. This myth according to Bazin was 'the great epic Manicheism which sets forces of evil over against the knights of the true cause'.[18] This is a description that, given that *The Lord of the Rings* films focus on the great good versus evil myths, would seem appropriate. Yet they are not Westerns. Rather, Bazin's approach is descriptive of the fundamental thematics that can underpin the motivation and appeal of some generic conventions; it does nothing either to account for the presence of such elements in other films/genres, how genre relates to the audience and industry, and on a deeper level how ideological tensions can be addressed by its codes. Robert Warshaw takes it one step further by asserting that again Westerns 'provide answers to, and seek to resolve in imaginary terms, particular needs and contradictions within American society'.[19] Yet once again how does this relate only specifically to one genre, and how does one separate such universal beliefs from appearing, say, in one text and not another?

In response to both these notions it appears that again we turn to the resonance and importance of film narrative in relation to myth as one of the most powerful carriers of meaning, an area often discussed in relation to spectatorship and semiotics in its own right yet often seen as an element informing genre but subsumed by it. What is important to remember here is that *The Lord of the Rings* films' familiarity, so often considered a vital element of audience participation in genre, is contained within the themes, narrative and character types offered as opposed to their stylistic qualities. Lawrence Alloway's approach to genre in terms of iconography is less easy to use in that the iconographies within the films are plural; however, his identifying of

'recurrent character types and situations which would become familiar to audiences through repetition' is another way of analysing the films.[20] Returning to prior assertions, however, it is hard to then differentiate these generic character types/familiarities from narrative structures and themes, the universality of which is so well demonstrated by the films in the previous chapter.

So, if using the traditional, established ideas of genre, *The Lord of the Rings* films are not the best example of genre films. This exposes some of the limitations inherent in genre theory itself. The films pose interesting questions about the fluidity and evolution of genre, the familiarity and hybridity of contemporary genre theory and its institutional context. The films do not belong to one generic category, but utilise small elements of many, balancing the familiar with the refreshingly new, calling into question both the nature of hybridity in contemporary cinema as well as the erosion of the traditional boundaries and therefore genre analysis itself.

While on the one hand the films do contain elements of the Western – for example, by 'making their canvas as grand as possible, they will…range across an extensive geography. The sweep of history and geography will also command the staging of events in the most sensational and spectacular ways possible at the time of their making'[21] – their narrative is more fundamental and universal than the small-town vs. wilderness themes so evident in the Western. While critics analysed that genre because its historic and geographical specificity seemed at odds with its universal popularity, the same cannot be said of *The Lord of the Rings* films. Some of their formal qualities may resemble the Western (for example, loners on horseback moving from town to town fighting evil) but they mobilise myth beyond that of the American West, and thus according to Bazin's theories, surely are not Westerns at all. That the films cannot be placed in a 'set' position in relation to these ideas is what

NOTES:

14. Neale, *Genre*, 1980
15. Hutchings, in Hollows and Jancovich (eds) *Approaches to Popular Film*, 1995
16. Bazin quoted in Cook, *The Cinema Book*, 1999
17. Bazin, in Hollows and Jancovich, 1995
18. ibid.
19. ibid.
20. Hutchings, in Hollows and Jancovich, 1995, p64
21. Lusted, *The Western*, 2003

makes them both difficult and interesting to consider in relation to genre. Of genre theory's three-sided triangle, with Text–Institution –Audience at each point, it is the latter two that here are the most pertinent and form the basis of the majority of the discussion.

GENRE AND *THE LORD OF THE RINGS*

Genre theory is generally considered to relate to Hollywood cinema. However, recent academic writing on genre has identified the problems with attempting to ascribe traditional generic models to contemporary post-classical cinema. A defining characteristic of this period is its attempt to appeal to as many audiences as possible and therefore increasingly refer to numerous genres within any one text. Genre theory has tended to focus almost entirely on classical Hollywood cinema, and in an era of the post-classical and the postmodern, can these ideals be a productive methods of analysis?

Firstly, can *The Lord of the Rings* be seen as Hollywood cinema at all? Shot in New Zealand (therefore not USA-centric) by a native New Zealand director, using British accents, local crew and effects houses with an international cast, to see them as Hollywood films is problematic. However, they were funded by a major US independent, New Line. That this was the case lends them some weight as 'independent' films in the fact that they are not, in the traditional sense, big studio Hollywood blockbusters (although as examined in Institutions, New Line Cinema is owned by the conglomerate Time Warner). In other areas, however, particularly in their marketing, release patterns and audience response, they bear the hallmarks of big studio releases. This factor is important when considering audience response (and is considered in greater depth later) but here it

calls into question the very issue of generic theory, which relates so predominantly to Hollywood cinema as whole. So in order to examine its generic implications and locate it within contemporary audience and theoretical definitions, it is acknowledged that calling it a 'Hollywood blockbuster' is problematic, while recognising that its release strategies, narrative structure and iconography are in keeping with much of the debates about the spectacle of Hollywood cinema.

Looking briefly at some genres that it could be argued are referenced within the films, we can identify aspects of **action/adventure**, **fantasy**, the **war film**, the **Western**, the **swashbuckler**, the **historical epic**, the **family film**, elements of **melodrama** as well as the recognisable cinematic form, the **trilogy**. Additionally, they are literary adaptations. Jackson and company have seemingly touched on many heterogeneous genres and created homogeneous films with their own internal logic due to their strong narrative drive and, because there are three instalments, could be argued to have established a new (at the very least sub-) genre. This duopoly of familiarity and difference is key to the generic interplay of New Hollywood. 'Genre bending'[22], the blurring of genre boundaries by, and increasing emphasis on, films offering multiple genre characteristics (and thus audience appeal), has been argued to be causing the erosion of genre as a whole. The contemporary trend is for films to move in cycles: 'If a film is made as a one-off, not fitting clearly into any particular genre, and it is a big success, it is likely to be copied or repeated. Similar films will be made. More will follow if these also succeed. If this proves to be a short lived phenomenon it might be labelled a 'cycle' rather than a fully-fledged genre.'[23] The trend in Hollywood to produce spectacular cinematic event films ensured that *The Lord of the Rings* was defined as such, allowing it to position itself as a mainstream release with a certain kudos precisely because it was *not* following a cycle – it was in effect *creating* one.

So how, if this is the case, does the first film render itself both familiar and unfamiliar at the same time? By narrative and character types, and through the use of spectacle in relation to an industrially defined form, the **blockbuster**.

Despite the problems with the term, *The Lord of the Rings* films can be defined as blockbusters. All three films were tremendously successful, had enormous cultural and industrial resonance and successfully appealed to global mass markets. The term 'blockbuster' highlights again some interesting tensions of using genre theory to analyse contemporary cinema. It is a term that in a sense says nothing of the thematic or stylistic patterns of a film, more about its likely budget, mass appeal and often in retrospect its box-office success. Therefore, as a term it relates more to industry and audiences than to formal qualities. A 'blockbuster' would seem to mobilise multiple genres to appeal to the widest possible audiences, will have a set place in the annual release schedules (often around holiday periods, for example) and is the most extravagant end of the movie-making spectrum, using huge budgets to create star-led vehicles driven by spectacle, thrills and product tie-ins. The term is often used as a derogatory description in terms of quality, describing cinema that appeals to the 'masses' and finds its audiences through its saturating marketing campaigns. As with many generic terms it can be used with little or no analytical perspective. The term 'blockbuster' is often applied to films after they are successful, which can entirely remove the prior industrial background. For example, the first *Matrix* film (1999), made for under $60m, would not have been considered a blockbuster until it generated vast theatrical and domestic viewing returns. It could be argued that the term 'blockbuster' is thus a reflective one. This at least is useful when looking at genre in contemporary cinema by focusing almost entirely on audience response.

NOTES:

22. King, G, *New Hollywood Cinema*, 2003, p118
23. ibid., p119

The Lord of the Rings films in this context clearly are blockbusters, with their vast box-office takings. But how does one account for the intricacies of the fandom associated with the films? They are not, for many audiences, instantly gratifying, easily-forgotten 'popcorn movies' so often described as blockbusters (though they may be to some). They not only present difficulties in describing what a blockbuster actually is, but whether, at the point of consumption, it is possible to sub-divide the over-arching term 'blockbuster'. Perhaps it is more appropriate to label the films 'cult blockbusters', a term first discussed by Thomas Schatz,[24] which allows for more emphasis to be placed on continuous audience participation than simply looking at the blockbuster as a cynical industry device. The closest relation to *The Lord of the Rings* in terms of its status as 'cult blockbuster' is the *Star Wars* trilogy, with its sustained fan base. It demonstrates perhaps the differences between the blockbuster label and a less derided, more fan-based term, the cult film. The latter categorisation would acknowledge *The Lord of the Rings* films' lack of big Hollywood stars, a feature very common in the blockbuster overall (and often a defining feature of specific genres). As discussed, while the star status of the actors would rise during the schedule of the three films' release, initially at least there were no 'lead' stars. What there were, however, were 'quality' thespians in some key roles – Ian McKellen as Gandalf (reminiscent of the casting of Alec Guinness in *Star Wars*), Cate Blanchett as Galadriel, Ian Holm as Bilbo and Christopher Lee as Saruman. These 'heavyweight' actors are also mostly British, and it is worth noting the absence of any obvious American accents in the entire trilogy, once more differentiating them from standard 'Hollywood' films.

A further problem with locating these films in relation to genre theory is that they were, at least for the release of the first film, an unknown generic entity, yet at the same time had an established audience. People knew of the books, but in relation to audiences this meant that while some may have had an intense familiarity with the subject matter, others would not, and this factor of literary adaptation could actually repel some audiences. An element of genre is its repetitive, recognisable nature, and arguably one of the most dramatic aspects of *The Lord of the Rings* films is their originality. It is their appropriation and mobilisation of multiple generic patterns (in particular industrial patterns) to render them familiar enough to audiences that highlight the changing nature of genre. Considering once more the importance of genre for allowing audiences a degree of familiarity to organise their viewing, the films may mobilise elements of several genres but the fact that *The Lord of the Rings* is three films brings to the fore the popular, well-known, contemporary form of the **trilogy**. An established cinematic code precipitated by some of cinema's most successful films – from *The Godfather* (1972–90) and *Indiana Jones* (1981–9) to the *Star Wars* trilogy – it could render an unfamiliar entity (one of the main points with the films is how the first film built an audience with no prior exposure, not the case with the other two, of course) fit well into a pre-existing cultural category. Here the use of spectacle, often derided for its dominance in the blockbuster, would be the films' most obvious textual appeal. In terms of contemporary (as opposed to traditional) elements of genre, there are some areas that can be regarded as sitting within the over-arching diegetic coherence of the three films.

Generic Elements of the Films

As with most big-budget spectacular 'event' blockbusters, *The Lord of the Rings* bears hallmarks of the action/adventure genre: 'Most contemporary or post-classical action films are indeed more or less hybrids, drawing on and combining generic plots, settings and character types from sources including science fiction, the Western, horror, the epic, war films, crime cinema and thrillers, disaster movies, swordplay and martial arts, even comedy.'[25] On the one hand, that the films are an adaptation of what is considered one of the greatest fantasy books ever written means that the themes and the diegetic world presented in the films offer far more depth and detail than a formulaic strict genre film. But they do contain a large number of action sequences and have comedic elements (usually in interchanges between Pippin and Merry, Legolas and Gimli). But how is the action/adventure genre defined?

'Action presents the story events of adventure in a particular (thrilling) way… Adventure bears much more explicit narrative expectations: we will follow the protagonist or protagonists on a journey or quest into the unknown territories of adventure space.'[26] Much has been written on action cinema in recent years and its emphasis on spectacle over narrative (discussed in Narrative) as well as its meaning for representation. Looking at the two definitions of these genres, *The Lord of the Rings* clearly displays large elements of both. There are many large action set-pieces, and the entire narrative is focused around a quest and the adventures and incidents arising.

The films, like the books, also belong very much within the fantasy genre. Tolkien's books are regarded as the inspiration for a large amount of fantasy fiction written subsequently and are still regarded as the leading works of the genre (interestingly Peter Jackson has now become a leading fantasy film auteur). A large and established literary genre (both for adults and more recently for children with cross-over adult appeal), it could be regarded as a genre in its own right due to its thematic concerns, but also its loyal audiences. Fantasy *films* are more problematic. 'Generically speaking, fantasy films englobe four basic categories: horror, science fiction, fairy tales and a certain

NOTES:

24. Stringer, *Hollywood Blockbusters*, 2003, p178
25. Tasker, *Action and Adventure Cinema*, 2004, p7
26. ibid.

Gandalf approaches Minas Tirith in one of many 'epic' moments

type of adventure movie (journeys to improbable places and meetings with implausible creatures). Fantasy *films* are about areas we "don't really know about" and, therefore, areas we do not see as real.'[27] The latter two sub-categories, of the fairy tale and adventure movie, are the most applicable to **The Lord of the Rings**, although it could also said to be 'fantasy horror'. As a genre, therefore, the fantasy film tends to form part of other, larger genres, or only work as a genre if split into sub-genres that will deal with problems of difference. Therefore is it a cinematic genre at all?

The Lord of the Rings is also an epic. Historically the epic is a genre of grand scale, and hence grand budgets, and while as with all popular genres their production is cyclical in line with audience tastes, a big failure can kill the cycle for long periods, indicating once more the gamble undertaken by New Line. The first film epic is generally considered to be the silent classic **Birth of a Nation** (1915). Much of today's blockbuster emphasis on

spectacle and action has been likened to the appeal of silent cinema in its reliance on visual elements. Other well-known figures associated with the cinematic epic include David Lean, director of **Lawrence of Arabia** (1962) and the epic battle scenes Jackson depicts also bear comparison to the portrayal of mass combat by Akira Kurosawa. Of note in contemporary Hollywood is the tendency towards postmodern intertexuality and self-reflexivity, which is, however, entirely absent from the historical or fantasy epic, and is therefore absent from **The Lord of the Rings**. The Hollywood blockbuster's tendency to use spectacle as one of its major selling points is due to spectacle's universal appeal – it can overcome language problems globally. At the time of major advancements in CGI technology came a new wave of disaster films in the 1990s, the apogee arguably being **Titanic** (1997). However, enactments of contemporary disasters were generally shied away from by studios in the immediate aftermath of the events of 11 September 2001. Disaster films and many action films (whose

plots relied on political or religious extremists as villains) were too close for comfort and not as 'escapist' as might once have been thought. If contemporary events were undermining contemporary settings what could be mobilised? The past, or alternative histories. Which, of course, could not have been known during the filming of **The Lord of the Rings**. But that the first film was so successful mere months after 9/11 could point to the desire in the audience to intensely immerse itself in a world, albeit with its own troubles and resonant themes, that was not ours.

As with many epic adventures the story may be centred on a quest narrative; however, the battle sequences and thematic conflict against would-be tyranny also incorporate aspects of the war film. Like the Western, war films emphasise sweeping iconography, grandeur and the employment of multiple minor characters as extras in scenes of scale and carnage. Thematically, 'Combat is either on a grand scale or on a small, even individual one… Comradeship is paramount.'[28] While there are two giant battles (at Helm's Deep and Pelennor Fields) there are numerous smaller fight sequences. It is perhaps the third film that most displays the characteristics of a war film, with expansive charges involving thousands of digital extras. As the war cries ring out in the battle of Pelennor Fields and outside the gates of Mordor, one is reminded of Henry V's Saint Crispin's Day speech at Agincourt.

As mentioned, it is the fact that the films were produced and released in a familiar industrial form – that of a trio or trilogy – that allowed for extra-textual audience familiarity. As discussed, comparisons between **The Lord of the Rings** films and the **Star Wars** trilogy were under way even before the first instalment of the former had actually been released. As Neil Spencer wrote in *The Observer* during the run up to the release of **The Fellowship…** , '…the creations of Tolkien and Lucas, the Oxford Professor and the California movie brat, have much in common. Both returned to

NOTES:

27. Hayward, *Key Concepts in Cinema Studies*, 1996, p93
28. ibid.

traditional story-telling at a time when their respective art forms were gripped by experiment. Both produced mammoth sagas that, give or take the occasional Elf Queen or kidnapped Princess, are boy's own capers. Both are conscious attempts to tap the wellspring of myth. Both have become massively popular while being derided by purist cineastes and literati.'[29]

'Operating within the genre of science fiction/fantasy film-making, Jackson and Lucas share sophisticated abilities for combining technology and mythology in the creation of authentic, self-contained alternate universes.'[30] It is the word 'authentic' here that relates most specifically to the emphasis on creation of verisimilitude and realism via iconography, mise-en-scène, etc. that renders each series so ripe for fan worship and cult status. What is interesting is that while the *Star Wars* saga can indeed be likened to *The Lord of the Rings* (a constant quest, a band of rebels, some very similar character archetypes), although in 'chicken and egg' terms the books came before *Star Wars*, it is entirely possible to consider that *Star Wars* ironically was an influence on the film version of *The Lord of the Rings*. Some moments in particular are reminiscent of Lucas' trilogy; for example in *The Return...* as Rohan's Rohirrim army have defeated the orc army at Pelennor Fields they are confronted by another oliphaunt-mounted army, looking similar to the approach of the AT-AT 'walkers' on the ice planet Hoth in *The Empire Strikes Back* (1980); and just as Luke Skywalker destroys a whole AT-AT, so Éowyn too weaves between the legs of one of the beasts and brings it down.

Both sets of films bear elements of the family film, another typical signifier of the blockbuster. This is more contentious for *The Lord of the Rings*, which contain much more bloody violence yet still earned a relatively low rating (the first was a PG, the other two 12A with warnings for violent content). This is more clearly visible in their release patterns,

annually at Christmas, as event films. As considered in the Institutions section, the release of *The Fellowship...* was almost head-to-head with the first Harry Potter film and there was much discussion in the trade press about the competition between the two. They were perceived in some ways to be appealing to the same audiences by being fantasy films. In reality, *The Lord of the Rings* turned out to be far darker and more violent, yet still maintained an appeal with younger fans in a similar way to the first *Star Wars* trilogy.

Finally, 'Different genres tend to appeal – or are assumed to appeal – to different sections of the audience. Science fiction, action, horror and war films are usually assumed to appeal primarily to male viewers. Romance, melodrama and costume pictures tend to appeal to women.'[31] Here genre theory moves to encompass theories of gender and spectatorship which work on a fundamentally industrial level (with studios often aware of these stereotypical genre practices in identifying the appeal of certain projects). Fantasy, also, is generally regarded as a male-centric genre although, particularly in relation to the literary genre, it is increasingly being reclaimed by women. But if this earlier statement is true, how did *The Lord of the Rings* appeal to female audiences, and how did it balance the power of action and spectacle with the emotional intimacy required for the story to succeed?

The presence of generic elements of melodrama should not be ignored: 'Characteristics generally associated with "melodrama" remain applicable to many Hollywood products, old and new: oversimplified moral conflicts between good and evil central characters, formulaic action and strong doses of emotion heightened by the use of music and other expressive devices.'[32] Here melodrama is a term that cuts across genre boundaries rather than re-appraising and re-assigning the term to describe a genre in itself of importance to the woman's film and

denoting relationship-centric narratives[33]. *The Lord of the Rings*, for all its gargantuan battle sequences and sweeping location shots is in essence a melodrama in the broadest sense, concerned with the triumph of good over evil at its core and emotional relationships pivotal to this quest, in particular the intimate triangle formed between Frodo, Sam and Gollum. Looked at in these terms melodramatic elements pervade even the most spectacular of Hollywood genres. Yvonne Tasker even asserts that action/adventure films in general 'are punctuated by lavish and spectacular action sequences in the manner of the musical',[34] again emphasising the cross-generic function that melodrama carries (melodrama and the female audience seen as being pivotal to the traditional musical, action cinema generally seen as providing viewing pleasure for male audiences). It also needs to be acknowledged that a standard characteristic of narrative in Hollywood cinema is the double causal plot-line whereby romantic subplots must be resolved in order to offer full, final resolution. Thus the 'melodramatic' elements of the films (in particular the heterosexual love story between Aragon and Arwen) and indeed of any films are not only generic, they are a fundamental facet of Hollywood storytelling.

What all of these musings indicate is that applying traditional ideas of genre to *The Lord of the Rings* is problematic, and that re-addressing the positioning of the films in terms of audience understanding of more industrial terms like the 'blockbuster' and 'trilogy' allows for a more plausible look at the films in relation to generic characteristics. It must also be acknowledged that *The Two Towers* and *The Return...* were the second and final parts respectively of an over-arching story, making them instantly familiar to audiences and allowing the producers to capitalise on the success of the first film.

NOTES:

29. Spencer, 'Mordor, he wrote...', *The Observer*, 9 December 2001
30. Shefrin, 'Lord of the Rings, Star Wars and Participatory Fandom', *Critical Studies in Media Communication* Vol 21 No 3
31. King, *New Hollywood Cinema*, 2003, p136
32. ibid., p183
33. ibid.
34. Tasker, *Action and Adventure Cinema*, 2004, p5

Auteur

Auteur theory, the study of the director as author of a cinematic work, existed as the leading approach in film criticism prior to the development of genre theory, which in part presented itself as an opposing methodology (simplistically put, focused on the audience and industry rather than the 'artist'). Auteur theory had actually been used in some form since the 1920s to look at the role of the director but it was in its re-invention that it is most familiar to students today. Starting as a polemic with which to reclaim certain Hollywood directors by the influential journal Cahiers du cinéma **and with which to examine their use of mise-en-scène and film style, it also became in a sense a manifesto against what those critics saw as the previous European cinema's greater emphasis on screenwriting rather than directing.**

Virtually since its emergence as a method of analysis, auteur theory has been problematised and discussed, and it still remains a contentious term with multiple meanings from different perspectives. One issue taken with the theory was that studying the 'creative' aspect of one particular 'genius' over another is subjective, as is looking at film purely as individual expression as an art form, not as a commercial medium. This may suit the analysis of European auteurs such as Godard, Truffaut and Buñuel who attempted to promote film as a progressive medium, but in such a pure sense it omits any Hollywood director working within the studio system unless they are 'chosen' to be worthy of analysis by a select few. But precisely what criteria would be applied to make them such, and by whom, immediately rendered the term and its use as highly subjective.

Looking at the director as the primary artistic and creative force behind films leads to two main issues. Firstly, they must display a distinctive film style (a 'signature' style); secondly, they must display specific thematic concerns across their work.[35] Both are considered, in the traditional auteurist approach, to be indicative of the director's personal vision. In particular this relates to art cinema directors, whose enigmatic use of restricted character knowledge often meant that the audience was identifying with the director's, rather than a character's, point of view. Godard's appropriation of just about any film style, from referencing the gangster genre to refusing to be bound by any rules of time or continuity (using long, discursive, location-shot hand-held sequences or jump cuts), is an example of the way in which personal style has a very real effect not only on a film's visual but also narrative structure. But in relation to themes, British/Hollywood auteur Alfred Hitchcock is perhaps one of the best examples, with his pre-occupation with voyeurism and spectatorship. So clearly, an 'auteur' by this definition can work within the Hollywood studio system, or, as with Orson Welles, become legendary for a refusal to pander to studio interference.

The industrial element, that films must be financed (increasingly with very considerable sums of money), is often overlooked by this type of text/art-based position. This was acknowledged in one of the many critiques of auteur theory. Even as far back as the 1950s key film theorist André Bazin, one of the leading forces behind the re-establishment of auteur theory and pioneer of genre theory, noted that 'the cinema is an art which is both popular and industrial'.[36] Auteur theory has endured, however, and as with genre is one of the primary ways in which contemporary cinema is promoted and categorised. Before looking at that, however, there are more issues to be examined in relation to the theory.

A further complication with the idea of director-as-auteur is that it also does not allow for the fact that many individuals are responsible for creating a film. For example, as Jeremy Points (2004) examines in relation to **American Beauty** (1999): 'Do we tend only to think of directors as auteurs and therefore overlook other equally important figures in the making of films – cinematographers, screenwriters, actors or composers for example?'[37] He discusses whether the auteur of that particular film could be argued to be scriptwriter Alan Ball (whose work certainly offers a certain verbal and thematic distinctiveness) or cinematographer Conrad Hall in place of director Sam Mendes. Jackson is co-scriptwriter and co-producer of **The Lord of the Rings**: what of his collaborators as auteurs, in particular his wife/partner Fran Walsh who has co-scripted and co-produced most of his work? And if Jackson is involved in the scripting of the films, how can he merely be defined as an 'auteur' by his role as director?

A good example of a similar paradox is Quentin Tarantino, often considered a contemporary auteur and renowned as a director. Yet in **Pulp Fiction**'s (1994) famous 'le Big Mac' scene between John Travolta and Samuel L. Jackson, it is the dialogue, his scriptwriting that is so distinctive. In the **Kill Bill** films (2003–4) the emphasis is entirely different. Both **Pulp Fiction** and **Kill Bill** demonstrate his penchant for non-linear narratives, black humour, deliberately stylised excessive violence and an eclectic soundtrack; however, in his latter films the plot is simple, the dialogue minimal and the emphasis far more on the playing with formal stylistic devices, including animation. His name as currency appears to grant him license to experiment with any thematic or stylistic elements he wishes. It offers a degree of familiarity when, generically, his films (**Kill Bill** in particular) are harder to categorise.

The producer and co-writer of **Pulp Fiction**, Lawrence Bender, might arguably be regarded as being equally important to that film's success, yet how many members of the public know his name? This is a further interesting tension of auteur theory in general – a producer is often the person who selects the director for a project. They are phenomenally

NOTES:

35. King, *New Hollywood Cinema*, 2003, p87
36. Bazin, in Stringer, *Hollywood Blockbusters*, 2003, p84
37. Points, *Studying American Beauty*, 2004, p75

powerful people, without whom many 'auteurs' would not have been discovered/created, yet they are almost entirely invisible to the cinema-going public, with the possible exception of the likes of Jerry Bruckheimer, über-producer of 'high concept' mega-hits. If a film poster reads 'from the Producers of…' it will often be the films cited that offer a reference point for the audience (be they action, horror or romantic comedy), and arguably this only happens if there is no 'name' director to highlight (the films of Bruckheimer being a fair example of this). Auteur theory may be riddled with contradictions, but it is thriving as a method of film promotion and audience comprehension.

Peter Jackson: A 'New Hollywood Auteur'?

So what of Peter Jackson? Is he auteur as director, scriptwriter or producer? What of the startling production design of the films by Grant Major and John Howe? Or the scriptwriting of Phillippa Boyens and Fran Walsh, the cinematography of Andrew Lesnee or Howard Shore's powerful, operatic musical score? It would appear that auteur theory allows for one artist to be revered by the public and utilised for promotion, when the very nature of film as collaborative medium calls the theory into question on many levels. Tolkien, as novelist and creator of Middle Earth, is also arguably the auteur of the films with his source text supplying the style and feel of the entire diegesis (the signature style and themes, as it were). The emphasis on one lone (and, more often than not, male) director would therefore seem to have less to do with the actual production process than the cultural and industrial processes through which film is understood. This issue of gender also calls into question the ideologically constructed, subjective nature of the image of male 'maverick' director.

It is far easier to examine auteur theory in relation to **The Lord of the Rings** films than genre theory. As we have seen it was historically regarded as an alternative that was less a prescriptive, subjective style of film analysis which could also incorporate the multitudinous other styles of film theory emergent in the 1960s, for example, structuralism and feminism. Looking at the 'purest' form of director as auteur, can we see stylistic and thematic concerns across Jackson's work? He had variously directed both cult and critical successes, his penchant for gleefully outrageous gory low-budget horror in films like **Bad Taste** (1987), **Meet the Feebles** (1989) and **Braindead** (1992) sitting alongside his acclaimed **Heavenly Creatures** (1994, launching the career of Kate Winslet) and the less successful but critically acclaimed Hollywood horror film **The Frighteners** (1996). On all he acted as screenwriter and producer simultaneously, and all could be said to have elements of horror, with him gaining a reputation as as a cult director particularly in relation to his early films.

We should also look at the production process of the films. Many crews were in entirely different parts of New Zealand shooting simultaneously, with Jackson watching footage via satellite link ups. This meant the use of individual Unit Directors to actually sit in the director's chair, as it were. So, in a 'pure', auterist sense, who is the 'author' of those scenes? Of course we could argue that it is still Jackson, whose vision those individuals were abiding by, but this does call into question the view that a director is unilaterally, solely responsible for a film's creation. As with many methods of organising and eradicating contradictions so often discussed in ideological terms in relation to cinema, here it would seem that the director-as-auteur mantle is used to smooth over such issues and create a logical coherence for its audiences.

Taking **The Lord of the Rings** as an example, Peter Jackson has become not only, in the

The avuncular auteur

contemporary sense, an auteur, but also a star. In today's Hollywood what arguably differentiates the 'name' director from the jobbing film-maker is power and public profile. Jackson not only set himself up as director of the films, but as co-producer, co-screenwriter, used his production company Wingnut Films, filmed in his own country, utilised his own special effects house (Weta) and his own studios (Three Foot Six). Due to the enormity of the budgets it was not a case of self-financing, but it looks very much like a form of artistic and, importantly, industrial control afforded to him. This is reminiscent of the directors with financial and industrial 'clout' who emerged from 1969 onwards during what became known as New Hollywood Cinema. At that time it was Hollywood rather than Europe that produced a group of ambitious, talented (male) directors/producers including Robert Altman, Francis Ford Coppola, Martin Scorsese and soon-to-be blockbuster kings Steven Spielberg and George Lucas. So, the idea of auteur now had an industrial angle to faciliate artistic control. Is this a re-appropriation of auteur theory?

NOTES:

Auteur

This style of film-making, particularly in relation to directors such as Spielberg (who, together with David Geffen and Jeffrey Katzenberg, established his own studio, DreamWorks), is seen as a new form of vertical integration by the individual. 'The business of being an auteur, in this context, is less a matter of personal artistic endeavour than of achieving a status that sells both the film to the viewer and the director of the studio.'[38] Jackson, seen in these terms, is indeed a New Hollywood auteur now; however, prior to the films being greenlit, merely a highly ambitious 'cult' director. Despite Jackson's eventual position of control, he still needed backers with deep pockets for such a costly project, thus auteur theory again is not adequate to incorporate the tremendous influence of studio bosses to either green light or reject projects. Robert Shaye at New Line, the man who said 'yes' to all three films and a relatively unknown director, took a gamble by bankrolling the productions. Without such a willing producer, the films could very easily never have been made, once again highlighting the shadowy 'behind the scenes' role of the, in fact, virtually omnipotent producer.

As with genre, auteur theory has increasingly become a short-hand marketing ploy to provide disparate audiences some familiarity with the product. Genre has permeated the cinematic consciousness to offer shorthand categories both for audiences and distributors with which to locate films in a familiar framework (discussed more under Audiences). Auteur theory may have been highly criticised for its focus on the creative individual, but certain directors' names carry enormous box-office weight and therefore in the interests of the industry, the auteur, or should it be the 'New Hollywood auteur', is thriving. As Geoff King (2003) points out, 'A Film By…' in bold typeface on film promotional material carries with it a certain set of codes which work with an audience to create certain expectations: 'An implicit auteurism remains a convenience for journalism and other film writing and publications, the director being a handy tag on which to hang discussion or analysis that often fails to question the assumptions on which it is based.'[39] What this statement implies is that what has become rendered common is actually still on many levels problematic. Directors such as Spielberg and Lucas still wield phenomenal power, alongside former 'indie' directors such as Tarantino. Directors are increasingly becoming stars in their own right, therefore is it possible to argue that their stylistic and thematic concerns (the necessary qualities traditionally used to define auteurs) permeate their bodies of work, or that their name ironically affords them the freedom to move from genre to genre with financial clout and much more autonomy over their own products? Either way it does not address the fundamental flaw identified with auteur theory, that film is a collaborative medium. Authorship may be an instantaneous, short-hand marketing tool but its role is still highly contentious. This is even more so with films that involve large numbers of special effects, where the responsibility for developing and creating these does not lie primarily with the director but a highly skilled art and effects department.

So in the vein of director-as–celebrity, Peter Jackson has gone from being a relatively unknown director (certainly not well known by the mainstream) to being what could be described as a 'New Hollywood auteur' in the space of his three-part version of **The Lord of the Rings**. This is due at least in part to his undertaking of making three films simultaneously, a feat never before attempted, let alone achieved with such success. Now sitting at the top of the Hollywood tree (the June 2005 issue of *Premier* ranked him as the most powerful person in the US film industry), Jackson commanded a fee of $20m for his remake of **King Kong** (2005, another fantasy/horror, perhaps offering some indication as to his generic placement as new auteur). It would seem like a meteoric rise, especially if one considers the three films as one (which is how much of the writing on the films wishes us to see them). Yet here again we have the dichotomy between artistic and industrial elements – they are, in fact, three films, and that Jackson hit the box-office bullseye with each one makes him the director of three phenomenally successful films in succession.

But once again we return to the question of whether he is an auteur – and does it matter? If looking at **The Lord of the Rings** films, *of course* they have similar thematic and stylistic hallmarks – it is essentially one (very long) film. And Jackson did indeed have an enormous amount of influence in many areas of the films' production. However, he himself has admitted that he is the 'public' face of the films, to save his collaborator and partner, Fran Walsh, from the media glare, as well as to preserve some form of normality for their family. As previously stated, where auteur theory remains controversial is where it potentially overlooks the influence of the screenwriter (the originator of all films and prior to the emergence of the auteur theory perhaps the most revered role in European cinema, at least) in favour of the director, and with Jackson what is interesting and lesser known is that he co-adapted Tolkien's work with two women, Fran Walsh and Philippa Boyens. In terms of auteur theory, from its conception to its reincarnation in contemporary Hollywood, it has almost always dealt with male directors and while this has been re-addressed by feminist critics, it is still of note here that while the actual production process was equally male and female balanced (or even biased to two female screenwriters and one male, and with some scenes also being directed by Walsh), the films are still seen overwhelmingly as Jackson's. Part of this may come from the ease with which his name and status can be appropriated to contemporary standards of auteurism in relation to 'maverick' male directors. And Jackson's awareness, and manipulation, of this exemplifies to what extent a director can now control their own image.

NOTES:

38. King, *New Hollywood Cinema*, 2003, p115
39. ibid, p111

None of this is to imply anything other than that Jackson was primarily responsible for mobilising the industrial elements to best artistically create the films he wanted to make. His status now is one of a tremendously successful film-maker, but also a cult one, with the films and his handling of them working on many different levels for different consumers (the DVD extended version and extras for cult fans, for example). As will be discussed in Audiences and Institutions, he made the effort to consult Tolkien devotees via the web during pre-production for the films, and therefore presented himself as both director and fan of Tolkien, and an approachable person rather than imposing authority figure, disrupting the powerful/lone auteur figure idea. He personally received Oscars for Best Director, Best Screenplay and Best Film for *The Return...* (largely perceived as awards for the whole project), the film taking eleven in total, every single category for which it was nominated, indicating that his artistic and industrial peers acknowledged the achievement. His allying himself with fans of the books and films allowed many to see this Oscar triumph as the victory of the auteur who saw himself as a facilitator of someone else's vision (Tolkien's) which along with his enthusiastic nature aligns him with his audiences as an 'everyman' (discussed later in comparison to George Lucas but also touching on the importance of star theory here, in the creation of an image that is both familiar and 'special'), yet who carries with him enough conviction and determination to succeed in a difficult industry.

Jackson, Bernard Hill and Viggo Mortensen on the set of *The Return of the King*

NOTES:

Themes

As touched on in Narrative, the themes of _The Lord of the Rings_ relate very much to fundamental polarities of good and evil, light and dark. The voyage (or arguably the odyssey) undertaken by Frodo and the other characters is a fundamental fight against evil, and thus elements of the folk and fairy tale sit right at the heart of the story.

One of the most significant themes of the films is myth itself. Middle Earth is a narrative space with enormous 'history', as demonstrated by the stories, songs, and vast exterior and interior sets echoing with the grandeur of the past. Tolkien's belief in myth was so fundamental that here it _becomes_ history. His interest in Anglo Saxon, Old Norse, the creation of new languages via the study of old and the influence of works such as _Beowulf, Sir Gawain and the Green Knight, Pilgrim's Progress_ and even _Paradise Lost_ are all evident in the creation of Middle Earth. This theme of myth is enhanced by Tolkien's use of both song and more regularly language. Middle Earth is a land of many languages, from Elvish to the language of Mordor, and these are used within the film. The use of subtitles may offer audiences an understanding of the actual meaning of the words being spoken but beyond that they may marvel at the complexities of the alien language they are hearing. It is of use at times in the narrative, but more importantly it reinforces Middle Earth's three-dimensional historical, cultural and linguistic development which all feed in to the dominant power of myth.

Tolkien's belief in myth was categorically not from a semiotic perspective. 'He saw myths as an expression of divine truth to which the imaginative inventions of art and literature could aspire.'[40] This ascribes myth greater weight as an absolute, rather than a cultural invention, and he clearly distinguished between the two. This may partly explain why his books do read less as fairy tales and more as accounts simply of a period pre-history.

It is widely known that Tolkien himself, as well as being fascinated with ancient stories and languages, was a devout Catholic. Despite his distaste for allegory, allegorical claims for his work have been made, especially its religious connotations. Unlike his close friend C.S. Lewis whose works were openly devout in content and meaning, Tolkien's works do not subscribe to one specific faith; however thematically, religious beliefs are visible throughout the story. The (Pagan) world of Middle Earth appears to exist without an organised belief system – it revolves around Kingdoms governed by mortals, with certain individuals and races endowed with mystical powers (the elves, for example). There is also the role of magic, which is shown as powerful and otherworldly and therefore again outside the confines of a particular doctrine. Many of the themes revolve around two primary areas – firstly the notion of states of being/levels of consciousness (from dreaming to purgatory) and secondly the idea of what it is to be human (ideas of free will and the individual regularly surface).

In terms of Christianity, taking Sauron as the devil figure, his nemesis is Frodo. Small, brave and embarking on a quest not only for his own salvation (not to succumb to the Ring) but the salvation of all of Middle Earth, Frodo could be likened to a Christ figure. He endures great suffering as the bearer of the Ring, suffering he undertakes for the sake of mankind, which evokes an unavoidable parallel. He is in effect 'resurrected' on several occasions: firstly, after he is stabbed by a Black Rider and saved by Elven magic; secondly, as he survives the attack of the cave troll; and thirdly, as he survives not only the sting of Shelob but ultimately the burden of carrying the Ring as well.

Resurrection is in evidence in relation to other characters – Gandalf is seemingly lost in the first film but is resurrected, and in a sequence in which he describes his journey in _The Two Towers_, we are teased with what

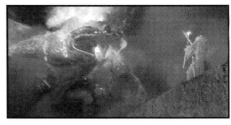

"You shall not pass!" Gandalf wards off the Balrog, prior to his 'demise'

must be glimpses of an afterlife, through stars and a white screen. This reference to the afterlife is then reintroduced in _The Return...,_ as Pippin is reassured by Gandalf that there is a paradise (heaven) awaiting them. Aragorn is similarly 'resurrected' after his fall from the cliff-face during the second film. There it is Arwen's love that apparently gives him life. In such ways death in the films is not an 'end' and thus plays with concepts of mortality.

In _The Lord of the Rings_, life and death may stand as the fundamental polarities, but between those are existences and other realities. 'The tale is... about Death, and the desire for deathlessness.'[41] Death suffuses the films, with the only defences against them being hope and courage. Mortality and brutality dominate the ferocious battle scenes; however, around these more familiar states are characters who are both undead and immortal. On several occasions characters are believed to be dead: Frodo (the most constantly threatened character of the trilogy); Gandalf, after his fall with the Balrog; Sam, almost drowning when attempting to swim to Frodo's boat in _The Fellowship..._; Pippin and Merry after the slaying of the Urak Hai; Aragorn, after his 'tumble off the cliff'; Faramir, about to be cremated by his father; and, finally, Frodo again (and Sam), as Mount Doom erupts. Some of these involve the notion of resurrection, while others are cases of mistaken belief. But all reinforce the tenuous nature of life and its proximity to death at all times.

NOTES:

40. Spencer, 'Mordor, He Wrote', _The Observer_, 9 December 2001
41. Tolkien quoted in Fuller, 'Kingdom Come', Film Comment, Jan/Feb 2004

Boromir falls, redeemed

Characters with flaws of varying degrees are offered **redemption** in death, again in religious terms meaning one must atone for one's sins before being allowed to enter heaven. Boromir, failing Frodo in *The Fellowship...*, dies redeemed for saving Pippin and Merry and accepting his true King (Aragorn, another potential Christ figure). Théoden, portrayed at times as a weak, indecisive and despairing leader, is allowed to redeem his honour by leading his people in battle. Even Gollum's malevolent scheming is in one sense redeemed as he in effect saves Frodo (and the quest) from himself by snatching the Ring and destroying both himself and it simultaneously (also reinforcing the Ring's ability to own weak personalities who succumb to its evil).

Continuing the theme of life and death there are various 'undead' characters that are in some form of **purgatory**. The Black Riders are tormented slaves to the Ring, who have in effect given their soul to Sauron (the devil). Their success is dependent upon claiming the Ring yet for all this there is never any implication that they will find peace – they have already chosen hell by accepting the Ring as their master. Although they are portrayed as corporeal beings, they are faceless and their true ghostliness is only revealed when Frodo puts on the Ring and steps into another reality. The army from the Paths of the Dead that Aragorn summons to fight in *The Return...* are also in purgatory for losing their honour in not fulfilling an oath. Once they have fulfilled it they evaporate into the air, presumably finally able to enter the afterlife having redeemed themselves.

Dreaming is another state of elevated reality employed throughout the films – Frodo 'dreams' of Gandalf's fall with the Balrog, and for Aragorn and Arwen their relationship relies on a connection between the two often symbolised by him apparently dreaming, or by her visions of the future (theirs being one of the relationships that confirms the importance of the ability to love as an overarching theme of the story). These moments 'provide ethereal respite from the films' thunderous blasts of warfare and the jaw-dropping phantasmagorical interludes'.[42] Gandalf's 'death' is also shown through the stars in a subjective montage to accompany his recollection; and Frodo inhabits another world with the Ring on his finger. In the 'real' world this renders him invisible (a characteristic of the Ring that is never fully explained), yet he has slipped into another dimension where he is visible to Sauron. With the Ring on, he (and we) can see Sauron's eye, see the Ringwraithes in their true and ghostly form and be seen only by them.

Along with dreaming blurring the boundaries of the concsious/unconscious mind, the idea of **seeing** and **perception,** of levels of consciousness is evident on a number of levels in the story. Frodo's perception of reality alters when he wears the Ring and at various points devices that allow some form of seeing beyond the physical world are utilised. In *The Fellowship...* Galadriel's 'mirror' shows Frodo the possibilities of events that lay before him, and as she states the mirror will show him 'things that were, things that are, and some things that have not yet come to pass'. This is in effect a refusal to confirm that the future is set in stone. And in fact even the wisest beings, for instance Galadriel, used as narrator and therefore imbued with a sense of superior knowledge in the mind of the audience, cannot actually see the certain future, only possible outcomes. This ensures a continuous instability to the narrative as well as emphasising the notion of human responsibility and intervention over fate and predestination. Pippin picks up the Seeing

Stone and is seen by Sauron. He is 'sensed' and also has a vision himself. Perception is linked with choice rather than inevitability, as knowledge rather than as absolute.

While this is certainly the case, the representation of evil, in the form of Sauron, could be argued to be an equivalent to the Devil. Sauron's desire is shown as a 'will to dominate all life'. **Power** is one of the most fundamental themes of the story. Sauron's power and will are manifested by the seductive nature of the Ring. Even an elf such as Galadriel, a creature straight from Milton's *Paradise Lost* not yet fallen from grace, is not immune to its powers. Power here equates with corruption, of the self and therefore of everything, as much is made of the importance and capacity of the individual within the story. Power and the Ring have been equated with the political climate in which Tolkien was writing, both before and during World War Two, hence it is hard not to see Hitler's tyrannical desire for domination being allegorised on some level.

Where Tolkien's more directly Catholic beliefs perhaps come through most clearly is in those characters guilty of **despair**. Despair is considered a sin in the Catholic faith, thus all those who suffer from it are repremanded – Théoden asks Éowyn not to despair, Frodo and Sam, as with many of the other characters, must embrace hope instead of despair in order to keep going, and Denethor, Steward of Gondor, the character who actually succumbs to despair (in *The Return...*) is driven mad by it to commit a further Catholic sin, suicide. Frodo's plight, as he hangs on to the cliff face above the fires of Mount Doom, presents him with a choice, and it is filmed in such a way that he may well let go and take his own life, but does not, and is ultimately rewarded by travelling to the 'Undying Lands' (an eternal heaven/utopia?). Despair is juxtaposed with hope, depicted as a very 'human' emotion that at times (near the end of *The Two Towers*, for example) imbues all

NOTES:
42. Fuller, 'Kingdom Come', *Film Comment*, Jan/Feb 2004

the characters. Hope requires belief, either in a higher power or as an individual, and although it has religious connotations it is also universal. Where there is hope there is also divinity and eternity, as represented by the elves. In a sense 'men' have already fallen from grace and the elves have not (tying in with ideas of Adam, Eve and *Paradise Lost*) and must therefore 'guide' (and help) them.

So while many of the underlying religious themes can be seen in relation to Christianity, the larger concerns of the narrative – the notions of choice and free will – are more fundamental moral issues. There is little mention of fate, and even the wisest characters, for example, Gandalf or Galadriel, cannot see the future as certain, only as a series of possibilities. **Love** and friendship are the overwhelming themes, with humanity and different forms of love (between men and women, men and men) standing as the polarity to the desire for power representing evil. Decency and the power of the everyman also feature heavily, with the physically small nature of the hobbits acting as a metaphor – it is their ability through inner strength, rather than physical, to overcome enormous evil. This is valour, and there is also continuous bravery and courage, the emphasising again of the moral strength afforded the individual. Many of the characters, in particular Frodo and Sam, are forced into a trajectory of innocence to experience (which could also be seen to be epitomised by Gollum at its most extreme). What connects all of the themes is their universality. The fully-fleshed world of Middle Earth for all its strange creatures is a place of fable or fairy-tale for its fundamental values of intrinsic goodness are exemplified in the actions of the characters and their plights.

Tolkien's experiences of war have also been identified by critics, seeing the story as an **allegory** (which Tolkien claimed not to believe in as a concept) of the Nazis in the build up to World War Two, and to his own experiences in the trenches of the Somme in World War

The Dead Marshes

One. Despite his disapproval of allegory few could see the Dead Marshes, with the long-dead faces staring up from beneath the water, as not in some way reflective of that dreadful historical moment and Tolkien's firsthand experience of it. Similarly the carnage-filled battles and overwhelming odds faced by the armies in the story as well as Sauron's will for supremacy reflect, deliberately or not, the horror of the Somme and the growing Nazi threat of the 1930s. Saruman's experimentation and breeding of a new race, the Urak Hai, could also be seen as redolent of the Nazis' cruel history of scientific experimentation as well as their belief in the dominance of one race (the world of Middle Earth is multi-cultural and multi-racial).

Critics have implied on varying levels that *The Lord of the Rings* is misogynist (with the majority of the principal protagonists being overwhelmingly male) and even racist. Representation of both gender and race is looked at in more detail in the next chapter but for now it must merely be observed that the books were written in the 1940s, and that Tolkien himself would most likely be appalled by particularly the latter accusation. There are ways in which the films transgress ideas of both.

Nostalgia is also evident in the films. Within the narrative, the location of the Shire is presented as the haven that Frodo, Sam, Pippin and Merry remember nostalgically. But in a wider sense, the ancient world represented by Middle Earth is a nostalgic harking back to a pre-technological 'other' world (albeit with the irony of only being filmable with the aid of modern technology) where the history is being told with such conviction and detail

that it seems real, but is not. By being a history that in reality belongs to no one, it can belong to everyone, and its audience appeal may at least in part have stemmed from this. One is reminded of the universalising mythology offered at the opening of the **Star Wars** films – 'A long time ago in a galaxy far, far away'. Here it is a different Earth. We can marvel at the presentation of 'history' and revel in the bloodiness of war possibly because it is at a safe distance, because this history it not ours.

The power of Hollywood cinema to cross cultural boundaries and create universally appealing narratives (as discussed under Genre) is also demonstrated by the films – they do not relate to any one specific national identity, but rather to multiple races and places all under the one unifying banner of 'Middle Earth'. As such they transcend the specificities that often prevent national cinema from travelling across borders and offer a tale of comradeship and uniting against a common threat. It has to again be mentioned that, even though the films had completed principal photography before the events of 11 September 2001, the portrayal of terrors unleashed on kingdoms and people, no matter how peaceful, could be argued to connect with contemporaneous anxieties over global terrorism. The films are able to offer seemingly inconsistent pleasures by being simultaneously escapist yet familiar enough to create empathy and verisimilitude by their attention to mise-en-scène.

Other thematic concerns bear parallels between the books and the films and their respective eras. For instance, Tolkien's distaste for the **industrial revolution** and its ramifications could be seen in Saruman's burning of the woodland in the name of industry. The black, smoking lands of both Isengard and Mordor are associated with coal and fuel-burning, of mechanical invention (e.g. the gate at Mordor, or the subterranean workplaces at Isengard) at the expense of the environment. These places are presented as

NOTES:

dystopias, juxtaposed against the natural world, rendered most stark when Treebeard sees his forest laid waste in *The Two Towers*. Concerns over industrial encroachment that infuse the books are echoed here in the films as the damage we continue to inflict on the environment is of increasing concern thanks to an organised ecological movement and discourse that did not exist in Tolkien's day. That the trees revolt and fight back is a startling idea. The Shire folk, with their peaceful existence in harmony with nature and its produce, are perhaps the embodiment of the rural idyll. **Nature** in the films is a powerful force – the places of mystical beauty are more often than not woodlands, metaphors for characters becoming lost in some way. And nature is angry at times – the power of the Ents is not only gratifying to watch but symbolic. With the enormity of the landscapes of Middle Earth constantly dwarfing its inhabitants, there is at all times a sense of man's insignificance and transitory existence in the face of an enduring landscape (for example, as Aragorn points out the magnificent Argonath statues, still standing long after his ancestors have died).

The emphasis for the entire diegetic world is around the elements of earth, fire and water (mentioned immediately in the opening prologue). Fire is associated with Sauron, and evil. Earth is the natural environments regularly depicted in the films, and water is not only the method of various part of journeys during the narrative it is also the force that destroys Isengard and the utopian sea on which Frodo departs at the end. It works therefore as a binary opposite to fire as evil.

Colour is used to symbolise good and evil in at times unusual ways. The 'Dark Lord' is just that and the 'evil' creatures, from the Black Riders to the Urak Hai in their armour (potentially where the accusations of racism come from when in fact blackness here is indicative of evil, a common cultural representation), are all dark to symbolise their role. Similarly the lands that are 'evil' are dark and fiery, with Mordor an ash-ridden wasteland (there is no greenery here, in keeping with the idea of evil working against the 'natural' order) or the smoke-billowing Isengard. The only green visible in Mordor is the luminous green of Minas Morgul, again associated with evil (this green is matched by the colour of the Dead Army). This is analysed in more detail under Locations and Settings but colour is of the utmost importance. The colour white is often used to signify purity, and indeed here it is worn by Galadriel, and upon the introduction of elves such as Arwen or Gandalf resurrected there is a blinding white light. However, this representation is undermined by Saruman the White, suggestive of more unstable representations of black and white as not at all times polar opposites but potentially two sides of the same personality (this accentuating the potential for even the most 'pure' to be corrupted).

NOTES:

Representation

The all-male Fellowship is formed

'Good stories tell good stories, whether they are about men, women or both.'[43] This may be true, but more interesting is how meaning and ideology are communicated through these stories. *The Lord of the Rings* trilogy is for all broad purposes, a story about men. The majority of the (many) characters are male, human or otherwise. The human race is described as 'the world of men', and it appears to be an ancient world where gender is biologically determined. They are also white. Tolkien's original work has been accused of being both sexist and racist, although neither assertion is particularly useful or appropriate; with the story being written in the 1930s and 40s it is inevitably a reflection of its time. However, he depicts characters (whose roles have been expanded by Jackson) who transcend their gender boundaries and similarly offers a world of multiple races united against a common threat. A more useful stance is to look closely at the three films and their representations of masculinity, femininity and race in relation to film theory debates both historic and contemporary.

Early feminist film theory and spectatorship theory asserted that gender boundaries on-screen were clearly defined and set. Mulvey's ground-breaking essay on *Visual Pleasure and Narrative Cinema* (1975), while offering a new angle and 'way in' to examining the representation and re-affirmation of patriarchal values, regarded the male as active and the female as passive, as object of the male gaze. This position of passivity was argued to mean that identification on the part of the spectator was with the active male protagonist, therefore bringing to the fore questions of the place of female spectatorship in such a male-centric medium as film, as well as the female depicted purely as sexual object on-screen.

These polarities have since been refined by, amongst others, Mulvey herself, and it has been accepted that the representations of femininity and masculinity on film are complex, with characteristics stretching across both genders to shift and redefine boundaries. Steve Neale's seminal article 'Masculinity as Spectacle' (in *Screening the Male*, 1993) began by examining in detail the process by which masculinity was also subject to voyeurism, including homo-erotic identification, opening up an enormous area of study in all forms of cinema, but particularly Hollywood. These areas are very much in evidence across *The Lord of the Rings* trilogy, with its presentation of a world similar yet distant to ours, striving for familiarity yet also distinctiveness within the diegesis and in its use of multiple characterisations. This will be examined in relation to particular characters under Masculinity in Middle Earth.

Much has been made of the male-centred world of Tolkien's Middle Earth. All the cultures/kingdoms represented are patriarchal societies and monarchies, with no democracies, and the threat of Sauron is in effect as a dictator. There is much emphasis on the bloodline of the males, with paternal background used to introduce characters – many are introduced as 'Son of'. This makes clear the importance of male lineage. The 'kingdoms' discussed are monarchies, and they are monarchies where the bloodlines are male, all with male kings or stewards (Theoden of Rohan, the Steward of Gondor and his two sons). However, they are in decline and dysfunctional, as we will discuss later.

The films and books have therefore been described (dismissed?) as 'boys' own adventures' by some critics. However, the sole prominent human female character, Éowyn, is not portrayed as happy with her lot, but as confined and frustrated, hardly a depiction of an idealised or fantastical femininity with its traditional roles being acknowledged as lacking (as we shall later see). As one critic wrote, the lack of female characters could merely be seen to indicate 'that Middle Earth still operates by the mores of 1930s Oxford'.[44]

The world of Middle Earth is multi-cultural, and also appears to be class-based. There are inter-racial love affairs (Aragorn and Arwen), friendships (Legolas and Gimli) and inter-class friendships (Frodo and Sam). The races are usually shown to be inherently either good or bad, with men occupying the middle ground. For example, at the highest level are the elves, then at the opposite end are the evil races such as the orcs and the Urak Hai. The Urak Hai in particular have been criticised for their appearance as potentially equating them with being black. While an admittedly sensitive – and valid – issue, this is an extreme reaction, with perhaps a more helpful response being to look at the the use of black to predominantly represent evil. This then becomes more about the cultural resonance of dark versus light and

NOTES:

43. Rusch quoted by Merritt in 'No Sex Please, We're Hobbits', *The Observer*, 7 December 2003
44. Merritt, 'No Sex Please We're Hobbits', *The Observer*, 7 December 2003

its implications; but it does not diminish the whiteness of the films and the books. The use of racial stereotypes has been criticised in films such as the second *Star Wars* trilogy (1999–2005), with the Jar Jar Binks character and his Gungan race in *The Phantom Menace* (1999) criticised as stereotypes of Jamaicans, or the ViceRoy in the same film being depicted as villainous aliens with Asian qualities. Such contemporary stereotypes are absent from *The Lord of the Rings*. So while it must be acknowledged that as with many contemporary films the explicit issue of race in our, as opposed to Middle Earth's terms, is omitted from the narratives, which arguably maintains dominant ideology by omission, it primarily signifies the source material's own context and limitations. That Jackson kept these ideas, as he did with the 'Savages' in his *King Kong* (2005) remake would make him a more appropriate candidate to ask about this issue than Tolkien.

Location has a bearing on race, and, as will be discussed in Film Language, the different races of men, in Rohan and Gondor, are differentiated by costume and appearance. Hobbits are portrayed as peace-loving, men as weak and dwarves as self-sufficient. The inter-racial bonds that form in the course of the narrative show that divisions are maintained around the opposition of good and evil. These are in keeping with the themes of uniting against a common threat, and the races associated with evil are framed and portrayed in entirely different ways to the individual characters of certain backgrounds.

As stated the monarchies, while being patriarchal, are also portrayed as in decline and ineffectual. In *The Fellowship...* there is a majestic scene as the Fellowship pass the Argonath, giant Kings carved from rock standing high over water. These nostalgic visions are in stark contrast to the monarchic ruin that becomes clearer as the trilogy progresses. As Frodo walks alone near the statues, he passes a stone King's head, lying

The Argonath - remnants of a monarchic past

broken and fractured, perhaps symbolic of the ravages that time has brought to Middle Earth.

In the case of the Kingdom of Rohan, King Théoden is under the control of Saruman and influence of the equally malevolent Wormtongue. As he sits decaying and passive, Rohan's people are being terrorised, his son is killed and his nephew banished. Gondor has only a Steward, with Aragorn the rightful king in self-imposed exile. While his son Boromir has a large part in *The Fellowship...* and Faramir is introduced in *The Two Towers*, the Steward himself is not present until *The Return....* He is shown to be mad with grief and unable to lead (resulting in Gandalf taking over the duty), filled with despair and eventually bent on infanticide and suicide. He is therefore an unfit leader and, as with Rohan, it is left to Aragorn to restore the order to its former glory.

Other references to this lack of the female involve several jokes made within *The Two Towers*. Gimli jokes of the similarities of the dwarf women to dwarf men, fuelling speculation that 'there are no dwarf women'. Similarly Treebeard, in the extended DVD version of the film, tells Merry and Pippin that they 'lost' the Entwives, the comedy in the fact that he means it quite literally.

What is of particular interest when looking at issues of representation in the films is how Mulvey's ideas can be both applied and problematised. It must also be acknowledged that by dividing this section into 'masculinity' and 'femininity' it is once more implying difference rather than interchangeability;

however, this does create a structure for the examination of key characters, raising interesting questions about the blurring of the lines of both.

MASCULINITY IN MIDDLE EARTH

As previously noted, what emerged in light of Mulvey's ground-breaking article was a clearly divided view of the 'difference' between masculinity and femininity on-screen. While males were seen as the active points of audience identification, female characters were relegated to being mere objects of a 'male gaze', both for the film's male protagonist, but also presented as objects for the audience. According to this argument there was little real pleasure to be had by female audiences who must either assimilate a male point of view (if it is so engrained in Hollywood cinema and wider society, this could itself seem 'natural') or identify with a powerless, passive object of the look.

John Ellis and Steve Neale, two critics interested in examining masculinity, rendered these polarities as ignoring the multifaceted nature of identification. Their arguments asserted that while masculinity had been identified as extremely problematic in feminist film theory, it had not been examined as an entity itself in any great detail. For both, the idea of identification being purely divisible into two static categories was unhelpful. 'Ellis argues that identification is never simply a matter of men identifying with male figures on the screen and women identifying with female figures. Cinema draws on and involves many desires, many forms of desire. And desire itself is mobile, fluid, at points even contradictory. Moreover, there are different forms of identification.'[45] These forms of desire are identified as dreaming and narcissistic identification which elevates identification above merely the socially constructed genders of

---

NOTES:

45. Neale, 'Masculinity as Spectacle', in Cohan and Hark, *Screening the Male*, 1993, p10
46. ibid., p11

Representation

male and female. Here it is located far more in the mind of the spectator and their sense of self.

What Steve Neale acknowledges, however, is that 'there is constant work to channel and regulate identification in relation to sexual division, in relation to orders of gender, sexuality, and social identity and authority marking patriarchal society. Every film tends both to assume and actively to work to renew those orders, that division.'[46] What is being argued here is that while identification is far more complex than looking at socially constructed gender roles, nonetheless these codes form for the most part the 'norm' in popular cinema. So how does one assert that one theory is more powerful than the other? And how can we see social roles as being ignored by audiences in their processes of identification? We need to look at both, and be aware that contradictions and paradoxes may be located between these arguments.

In relation to Mulvey's argument, her identifying the male protagonist as the audience's primary point of identification is obvious in relation to **The Lord of the Rings** – all the main characters are male. However, there is no sole protagonist, the films are ensemble pieces. The masculinities represented within the film are just that – multiple. They are also, for the most part, active, in particular characters such as Aragorn and Boromir whose masculinity is the most easily identifiable as relying primarily on external displays of strength and bravery. Neale's argument extended to look at both the embodying of certain 'traditional' masculine characteristics and also feminine ones, in particular the presentation of the male body. It is in relation to these arguments that the masculinities presented in Middle Earth can be examined.

Aragorn

Aragorn is the most traditionally masculine hero of the story, displaying all the competence in battle and combat to code him as physically strong through his actions, thus through

external factors, recognised by Neale to account for the presentation of 1980s masculinity as 'increasingly a vehicle of display – of musculature, of beauty, of physical feats and of gritty toughness'.[47] On many occasions the audience can relish Aragorn's single-handed dispatching of multiple creatures, which begins as he rescues Frodo from the Black Riders, firstly at Bree but more dramatically with his sword on Weathertop in **The Fellowship...**, where he is shot in slow motion (which he often is) fighting all of them simultaneously. He is coded, in terms of narcissistic identification in the audience, as the viewer's (aspirational) point of identification. During the numerous action set-pieces the camera follows Aragorn as he defeats his foes and it is his fighting skills that are foregrounded more than any other character. (The violence of some of the fight scenes tends to be shown more graphically in relation to Aragorn; for example, as the Fellowship fight the orcs in the Mines of Moria he is shown decapitating a foe.)

He is shot again in slow motion, as he overcomes a near-army of Urak Hai at the end of the first film, and it is he for whom the audience cheers in dispatching Boromir's killer (once again by decapitation). In **The Two Towers** his physical strength as well as leadership qualities are expanded, particularly in the Helm's Deep climax, where again his acts are shown as far more bloody than those of either Legolas or Gimli. But he is also shown leading the army and in keeping with Neale's notions of masculinity as spectacle, attempting acts of bravery including jumping on a ladder into the Urak Hai army and along with Gimli overcoming multiple Urak Hai outside the Deep doors. These moments of excess code Aragorn as omnipotent (excess is permitted for other characters such as Legolas in the 'skateboarding' moment) which deepens further in the third film when only he can summon the Dead Army.

So the pattern continues (and increases) for each film. However, the revelation of his true

identity as heir to a kingdom half way through **The Fellowship...** is depicted in a way to underline and make sense of his leadership qualities. This can be interpreted in two ways: firstly, that his bravery and fearlessness stem from his 'noble' lineage. But this is undercut by his counterpart, Théoden, displaying a lack of leadership and judgement. So Aragorn's external displays of strength and power could be said to stem from an internal source. Or as Steve Neale discusses Reaganite masculinity as about repetition and external display, he locates a shift in the 1990s towards a more internalised dimension – 'More film time is devoted to explorations of their ethical dilemmas, emotional traumas, and psychological goals'; however, he then says the effect of this is 'less to their skill with weapons, their athletic abilities or their gutsy showdown of opponents'.[48] But surely Aragorn shows signs of both? His internal struggle focuses on the failure of his bloodline following the seduction of his ancestor Isildur to the 'power of the Ring'. This awareness of his own fallibility is actually then a strength, emphasised by Boromir being physically strong but emotionally 'weak' for himself succumbing to the Ring. Physical strength is not enough, which ties in with a fundamental theme of the whole story, the different types of courage and bravery found within the individual.

So this internal dimension emphasises Aragorn's qualities as a 'new man' as Neale would put it, yet his displays of strength so gratifying for the audience complicate him as being both a traditional and a more progressive character. A further area of interest is in his presentation to the audience. He is the only male character to have a continuous romantic storyline (Sam is the other character to be 'rewarded' with marriage at the end of the films, which will be examined later), confirming his status as heterosexual hero. He has not one but two women desiring him, and while it is Arwen with whom he has a partnership, it is through the eyes of Éowyn that the audience often witnesses Aragorn.

NOTES:

47. ibid., p245
48. ibid., p245

As mentioned, in voyeuristic terms Aragorn is the narcissistic point of identification for the audience. This needs to be further explored. If Mulvey's original argument were applied to **The Lord of the Rings**, Aragorn would be the male protagonist most likely to be seen as the 'active' male with whom the men in the audience would 'identify'. This would leave little space for the female viewers in that the films and books have few female characters (which we will return to): 'Narcissism and narcissistic identification both involve phantasies of power, omnipotence, mastery and control. Mulvey makes the link between such phantasies and patriarchal images of masculinity.'[49] So in Mulvey's psychoanalytical terms Aragorn is the point of recognition, the 'subject', as it were. Where this argument becomes more difficult is in her denial of the male as potential erotic object as well as omitting potentially constructive cross-gender identification.

Aragorn is photographed as a source of both identification and objectification

'As the spectator identifies with the main male protagonist, he projects his look on to that of his like, his screen surrogate, so that the power of the male protagonist as he controls events coincides with the active power of the erotic look, both giving a satisfying sense of omnipotence.'[50] This may account for male identification with a character such as Aragorn, but not female, which is where examining the social constructs of masculine and feminine qualities and their interdependence becomes more useful in allowing female audience members to identify with Aragorn. Similarly in disavowing such a protagonist as the object of the look this removes a further dimension of how he is framed as a character.

Along with bravery and courage being signature characteristics of **The Lord of the Rings**, another defining element of masculinity (and here it goes against the individualist narratives observed by Neale, *et al.*) is companionship. Examined in Themes, it is worth repeating here. But comradeship is the realm of men alone – none is displayed between any of the women, who are isolated or surrounded by

men. It must also be noted that the type of masculinity embodied by Aragorn is evident in other male characters in the films – firstly Boromir, discussed in relation to his emotional 'weakness' but who also demonstrates bravery in combat, as does Éomer of Rohan, and perhaps to a lesser extent Faramir, whose dysfunctional father Denethor is yet another example of a failed patriarch in the story. And of course the Fellowship characters themselves, while not being men, are also brave and heroic – Legolas, Gimli and Gandalf, whose powers elevate him beyond this traditional archetype yet he fights in combat alongside the others. It is Legolas and Aragorn, however, who remain the two characters framed most often as 'spectacle' in the combat scenes.

Much has been made of action cinema in relation to the potential homo-eroticism of the presentation of the male body. Yet the genre's popularity with men could be seen as the denial of the pleasures of voyeurism in favour of identification. Aragorn, while being depicted as an active male protagonist and established as

a point of narcissistic identification, is also subject of the erotic look. While his body is not displayed but covered (unlike Frodo, also subject of the erotic gaze), his depiction does not disavow the look but at times actively shows him as the object of a female or homo-erotic gaze. The two most obvious moments of this are in **The Two Towers**. As he accompanies the people of Rohan towards Helm's Deep and they are attacked, the women, led by Éowyn, must continue while the men stay and fight. Denied her chance to fight and by now clearly attracted to Aragorn, it is from her point of view that we see Aragorn mount his horse in slow motion. We are witnessing him entirely from her point of view, and this is magnified by the slowness of the image. Aragorn (and actor Viggo Mortensen) is thus presented as object of desire for Éowyn but also the audience (meaning she is the bearer of the 'look', traditionally associated with male protagonists). What is interesting is that this does not place him in a position of passivity – he is still active, and actually looks back directly at Éowyn, thus

NOTES:

49. ibid., p11
50. Mulvey, 'Visual Pleasure and Narrative Cinema', *Screen*, Vol 16, Pt 3, 1975

matching her look (she has previously been shown in slow motion from his point of view). He is also shot in slow motion arriving after his 'resurrection' at Helm's Deep, opening two heavy doors (this was interestingly used at the end of the film's trailer, indicative of the image's impact). So once more he is potentially the object of the look.

So what does this mean? To answer that fully we must examine other characters and their traits, but in relation to Aragorn it should be noted that his power as active male or erotic object are not exclusive, giving weight to the argument that both masculine and feminine traits can move fluidly and be encompassed by characters regardless of gender. It also points towards an egalitarian gaze for the films; it could be argued that there is objectification of both male and female characters. Legolas and Frodo are both also considered objects of a female/homo-erotic gaze. What complicates this is the issue of narcissism and the homo-erotic look commonly cited in relation to masculinity as spectacle. Aragorn may be subject of the look but he is also confirmed as the heterosexual hero (unlike the other two) by his eventual union with Arwen. Along with Éowyn this may suggest a way of seeing Aragorn as narcissistic point of identification for both male and female and object of a female gaze. Interestingly, while he is both active and object of the look, Aragorn is also 'rescued' by Arwen in *The Two Towers* after his fall from the cliff. That the rescue is depicted in terms of dreams or visions leaves it open to interpretation however, and ultimately his omnipotence is reinforced rather than undermined by this scene. It is likely that such elements vie against each other and offer multifaceted and at times contradictory views of the ideological implications of representation. The actor Viggo Mortensen, while a relatively recognisable supporting actor, was previously not a star whose 'persona' would interfere with his character within the narrative (the codes of stars often 'exceeding' their characters within any particular film by

introducing extra-diegetic cultural references). With this in mind we will turn to the other and perhaps more central 'hero' of the story, Frodo, with reference to his pivotal relationship with Sam.

Frodo

Representing different forms of masculine strengths that rely on an 'internal' dimension is Frodo. He is ultimately the hero, the one dispatched on the quest. Whereas the Ring is seen to corrupt weak men, Frodo as a pure-hearted Hobbit is deemed the most likely to succeed in resisting the power of the Ring, implying his strengths to be something other than physical. This resistance wears thinner and thinner and is perhaps most frighteningly rendered in the prologue to *The Return...* where Gollum is shown to resemble Frodo in his life before the Ring, as Sméagol. His size, as with the other hobbits, means he is out of place and vulnerable for the majority of the film. It also, in full length shots, renders him child-like in stature and therefore vulnerable and needing to be looked after (at times the hobbits are carried by other characters). He is also rescued at several times, potentially undermining his status as masculine hero, or, viewed more progressively, embodying a more fluid view of masculinity to encompass vulnerability. Of particular interest here is that although his 'struggle' within the story is internal, his body is the most attacked, injured and also arguably objectified of all the characters.

In psychoanalytical terms Frodo is both penetrated and castrated. Feminist film critics who have utilised psychoanalysis to examine the voyeuristic pleasures of the male gaze have identified the prominence of acting out fears of the subconscious. Much has been made in relation to horror films of the nature of their use of knives as weaponry, in that stabbing is both penetrative and more intimate than other forms of weapons. Frodo is attacked by 'unnatural' monsters, and is constantly under threat, from the Black Riders, and all manner of creatures. He is stabbed (i.e. penetrated) on

several occasions. Firstly in *The Fellowship...* he is stabbed by a Black Rider on Weathertop and almost dies. His only hope is through his rescue by Arwen, which is a reversal of traditional gender roles. He is then speared again, this time by a cave troll during the fight scene within the Mines of Moria. That time however he is forearmed and is secretly wearing Bilbo's protective armour. Most pertinently, in *The Return...* he is again penetrated, this time by the sting of Shelob the spider. As the name suggests, this creature is female. She is the 'monstrous feminine' incarnate (as discussed at length by feminist critic Barbara Creed). Her lair, a cavernous place of death shot as a tunnel, could be argued to be a metaphorical vagina or womb which equates here with death. 'Freud's discussion of the uncanny (unheimlich) is relevant to the depiction of uterine imagery…he defines the uncanny as that which "is undoubtedly related to what is frightening – to what arouses dread and horror".'[51] This can be extended to involve 'losing one's way' which again is the case as Frodo enters Shelob's lair. That Frodo is covered in the sticky bodily fluids of the spider is another potential reproductive reference, and once he is actually penetrated he must again be rescued, this time by his companion/helper (and fellow hero of the story) Sam.

Ultimately he is 'castrated' by Gollum, who bites off his finger. In relation to psychoanalytical theory again the castration fear can be acted out through 'dismembered limbs'.[52] It is after this point in the narrative, once the Ring has been destroyed, that Frodo almost chooses martyrdom, as he hangs from the precipice in Mount Doom, in a moment rich with religious connotations. He eventually rejects this and survives; however, he is permanently marked by several of the attacks on his person. His body is a site of meaning in a different way to the other male characters, in that far from his body being used to connote strength and omnipotence, as could be argued with Aragon, it connotes vulnerability. Frodo's

NOTES:

51. Freud, 'The Uncanny', quoted in Creed, *The Monstrous Feminine*, 1993, p52
52. ibid., p53

further transgression is that he is the only member of the entire Fellowship, indeed the only character at all, shown naked. While for many of the other characters their wearing of body armour impies they are physically impenetrable, Frodo is significantly vulnerable. As he lies in the Tower of Cirith Ungol following his stab by Shelob, he is naked (shown from the chest up) and tied up, with both his wounds and his body on visual display. Not only does nakedness here equate with vulnerability it lays him open to objectification. From this state, he is rescued.

Also of interest are the potential meanings behind the choice of phallic weapons – a sword, a spear and a sting. The weapons (as with all the film's mise-en-scène elements, adding to the 'authenticity',) are pre-technological. Swords allow for extended fighting sequences where guns, for example, would not (see Weaponry and Props in Film Language). Such sequences can heighten tension, but there is also something very personal about stabbing weapons, they are deeply penetrative and are extensions of the body, animalistic and primal. Frodo is penetrated, and in the case of the spider, is penetrated by a female.

In relation to identification, it is Frodo's face which alongside Arwen and Éowyn personifies the horror and potential despair of the story. He is often shot in close up and extreme close up, with emphasis on his eyes, which become increasingly like Gollum's as his spirit begins to wane under the influence of the Ring. It is his expressive face that encapsulates the grief and hopelessness felt by everyone at the loss of Gandalf outside the Mines of Moria, and his face continues to be used heavily in the melodramatic sequences that highlight character-based drama and intimacy in the face of the enormous battle scenes.

The relationship between Sam and Frodo is undoubtedly the most intense of the story. The pair and their journey with Gollum form

Frodo is often shot in close-up, emphasising his expressive eyes

the melodramatic emotional core of the story. Sam's devotion to Frodo is clear throughout and the affection the pair feel for each other becomes more and more pivotal. Peter Jackson's refusal to downplay the potentially homosexual subtext of such an intense relationship leads to a storyline open to multiple interpretations or oppositional readings. It is an inter-class relationship – thus the emphasis in the earlier part of the story of Sam referring to 'Mr Frodo' demonstrating Frodo's superior social status. Frodo's clothes are also made of fine cloth, and he is the only hobbit to speak the Queen's English without a regional accent. Their 'friendship' is therefore based on something else. What that is can be opened up to examination.

The open-endedness of the storyline is interesting because it goes against the disavowal or closing off of an oppositional reading that one would frankly expect in a big budget film – 'assuming that all characters in a film are straight unless labelled, coded or otherwise obviously proven to be queer',[53] – with classical Hollywood narrative working to affirm dominant ideology. This highlights the

way in which assumptions are made, and contends meaning as being in the realm of the spectator, who is influenced by the ideological tendencies of (particularly Hollywood) cinema to attempt to eradicate and disavow such readings as being contestable and potentially more progressive. Oppositional readings can be found in diverse ranges of star images and films from **The Silence of the Lambs** (1991) (and Jodie Foster herself) to **Thelma and Louise** (1991), **Gentlemen Prefer Blondes** (1953) etc., not to mention the 'macho' action/buddy genres. What these allow for is the fluid nature of constructed meaning and appropriation and the active role of spectatorship.

So in terms of Frodo and Sam, the moments the pair display mutual affection and concern are many – from Sam's devoted near-drowning at the end of the first film to follow his 'master', to the increasing tension between him and Gollum for Frodo's 'affections'. Sam is shown to understand Frodo in a way that no one else can, and his ultimate rescue of Frodo and their subsequent embrace as Mordor crumbles around them emphasises the affectionate bond between the characters. Even

NOTES:

53. Doty, *Flaming Classics: Queering the Film Canon*, 2000

though Sam is the hero rewarded with heterosexual union at the end of the films, the departure of Frodo (who kisses his forehead) only serves to reinforce the strength of the love between them. Many argue against a queer reading, as one might expect. But what it highlights is the potential for multiple meanings to be found within a storyline particularly if it is left fairly open-ended. Those that argue against this reading say it is about a friendship love. But this is surely in itself an interpretation. What an oppositional reading does is allow us to see that presumptions and assumptions can be unpicked and shown as just that. How a spectator chooses to interpret the events presented is therefore an active creation of meaning by the spectator rather than a passive receiving of it.

Frodo and Sam - open to interpretation?

FEMININITY

We have established that merely seeing the male protagonist as active and the female as passive can be complicated by revisions based around screen representation of both masculinity and femininity. As previously noted the films are predominantly about men and therefore the focus is towards the functions and contradictions of masculinity. This argument can be further explored by examining the female characters in the film, of whom there are few. Often female extras are used to elicit audience sympathy and anticipation, for example as the Urak Hai arrive at Helm's Deep the editing juxtaposes their ferocity with the terrified (blonde) women and children in the caves. This utilises traditional notions of 'women and children first'. To find more

progressive representations of femininity we must look to the few major female characters. There are three – Galadriel, Arwen and Éowyn. The first two are elves, with only Éowyn being a human female, and she is perhaps the most isolated but also transgressive character in the films. She must be located, as with masculinity and debates about the 'new man', in relation to the phenomenon of the cinematic action woman. (It must also be remembered that there is a fourth female character, the 'monstrous feminine', in the form of Shelob the spider.)

It has been established that the world of Middle Earth is overwhelmingly one of men and male power structures which we can now examine more closely. Firstly, the monarchies depicted have no Queens, with no explanation offered for their absence. Even where the characters involved are female (Éowyn and Arwen), both are seen in relation to either their father, as with Arwen, or their Uncle and father figure, as with Éowyn. Neither has a mother, thus both are defined by their relationships to men. It is of note that there is a lack of mothers across the films – Frodo has a father figure in Bilbo, but no mother. Femininity would seem to equate with isolation. Notably the one female who appears powerful in her own right is Galadriel, clearly the equivalent of a Queen in her realm, and therefore isolated in an entirely different way – by her power rather than lack of.

What this indicates is that patriarchy is very much the dominant structure of Middle Earth, with the exception of Galadriel. However, does any sense of her 'power' become undermined by the presentation of women via the male gaze? Looking at femininity from Mulvey's point of view, the female characters – Galadriel, Arwen and Éowyn – are very often shot clearly to be admired. Lovingly illuminated, costumed and beautiful, the entrances of Arwen and Galadriel are particularly pertinent as we are viewing them from the point of view of one or

more of the male characters. Both Galadriel and Arwen are introduced to us in **The Fellowship....** In Arwen's case we see her first holding a sword to Aragorn's throat in mock aggression (although this means he is temporarily vulnerable to the 'castrating' female); then in dazzling light, in slow motion as she approaches a wounded Frodo, thus he is our point of identification. When we meet Galadriel (having already heard and seen her in the prologue) as the Fellowship arrive at Lothlórien, once more the camera lingers on an illuminated Cate Blanchett in slow motion (and soft focus it appears), on her (white) flowing outfit as well as her face. The Fellowship for the most part stand enchanted by her beauty, so that once more a female character is being directly 'looked at' both by the audience and within the narrative. Her beauty is also being elevated and manipulated to a degree that renders it heightened, as with Arwen. What this implies is an impossibility of beauty to be gazed upon /worshipped by the men. What is of note, however, is that the nature of any gaze in the films does not at any point break the female body into parts and therefore objectify/sexualise the characters – the romanticism of their costumes is beautiful rather than sexual, with the characters remaining for the most part under cover.

Although the audience are first introduced to Éowyn before she meets any of the Fellowship, her beauty is presented very differently than that of the other, non-human, women. Firstly, of course she is a mortal human; therefore the otherworldly beauty ascribed to the other two females is absent. She is shown as isolated and watched by a malevolent Wormtongue (an unwelcome gaze which at one point she meets, looking back in anger, making us complicit voyeurs). However, as the Fellowship arrives at Edoras in **The Two Towers** it is Aragorn who sees her as a figure all in white, standing in the wind. Not only are the audience looking at her face filled with despair in close up but her whole body (and costume) stands out (which ties in with elements touched on in Film

NOTES:

Language, that the female characters are highly adorned and less functionally, more romantically dressed than their male counterparts).

So it is true that the ways in which the female characters are depicted is often for their beauty and their to-be-looked-at-ness. However, where this argument becomes more complex is that the female characters are not the only ones to be the subject of the camera's voyeuristic gaze, neither are they merely passive. We might continue to adopt a more fluid appropriation of Mulvey's theory, that feminine and masculine traits can be applied to characters of both genders. For example, Galadriel, despite being lovingly depicted by the camera as an almost angelic being, is also shown in the narrative to be far wiser than those around her and it is for this that she is revered, not her beauty. She becomes, as do so many of the characters in the story, Frodo's helper as well as another dispatcher. Her wisdom is established during the prologue to all three films when she is the narrator of the story of the Ring. Although her assistance is not as dramatic as that of the other two female characters, she remains a constant, powerful figure of knowledge throughout the story who by her immortality is an interesting dichotomy of youthful (eternal) beauty and wisdom. (Cynically, perhaps, one might say women here are not *allowed* to be, or appear, old, like Gandalf, but must maintain their beauty *and* amass knowledge.) She is also the most 'powerful' female, as a leader, not shackled by her relationship to men (however, this could be said to be nullified by her not being human, or show a matriarchal utopia within the freedom of 'displacement').

The first 'active' feat of any of the female characters is Arwen's. Following Frodo's stabbing on Weathertop in the first film she arrives and takes him to Rivendell, chased by the Black Riders. Her strength is contrasted against Frodo's vulnerability (he is very small and near-mortally wounded) and as she

reaches a river and turns to face the Riders the framing of her on her horse, sword drawn, horse on back legs, is powerful in its defiance, as is her summoning of the river to rise up and swallow her foes (an act not performed by Arwen in the book). Her 'strength' here shifts – having started off physically adept at riding, her power then transfers to be more spiritual, which is how she stays for the remainder of the story.

So does this mean she is still powerful? Certainly it can be argued that she psychically/magically 'saves' Aragorn following his fall in *The Two Towers*; however, her rescue of Frodo is the only obvious physically progressive act on her part. She is increasingly caught between men: her father (in what could be read as an Oedipal subtext, who desires her to take the journey 'across the sea') and Aragorn, the mortal whom she loves (an inter-racial romance, as it were). Offered a vision of a life after Aragorn's death, where she carries on a grieving widow, she does agree to leave Rivendell, but sees another vision on her way. This time it is of Aragorn and her son (Aragorn's heir). Again we can observe that the films' world revolves around fathers and sons, with Arwen's allegiance moving from her father to her new 'master', Aragorn, with her acting as an object of exchange. This means that despite being an elf, she is still very much contained within a patriarchal society, moving from obedient daughter to devoted wife and mother, all terms that indicate her relative status to the men around her. It has been noted briefly that Arwen in particular is shown caped and bowed in the manner of the Virgin Mary at various points, with even a blue shroud. The religious reference and the deference in which the immortal females are held and worshipped is much like the unattainable beauty and otherworldliness embodied by the Virgin Mary in the Catholic faith.

It is Éowyn who most challenges the confines of her role and who is most deserving of our attention. However, it must be noted that the

film's two biggest international stars were two of its female leads, Cate Blanchett and Liv Tyler. While the ensemble nature of the Fellowship requires no one star persona to jostle for status or disrupt the narrative, the two female elves are well-known. That they are also presented as 'special' within the film and the world of Middle Earth through their immortality and grace, may go some way to explaining why their star power does not greatly affect the 'realism' of their performances. They are worshipped and unattainable in a strange mirroring of the impossible appeal of stars themselves, and interestingly this is not the case with Éowyn, the sole female human of any note. Played by Miranda Otto, a relative unknown, she is on the same level playing field, as it were, as her male counterparts. Perhaps this warrants her the most freedom away from any 'male gaze' or at least to appropriate more active characteristics.

Éowyn

While Arwen and Galadriel may be presented as adored creatures, Éowyn is almost totally isolated. Unnoticed by her bewitched Uncle, her brother banished and cousin dying, her despair and loneliness are established very quickly upon her introduction in *The Two Towers*. Following her dramatic entrance standing on top of Edoras for Aragorn to see (as well as for the audience) she is shown practising with a heavy sword. This is interesting because it is a very 'masculine' weapon (examined more closely later). When she literally locks swords with Aragorn (matching him at his level) she talks openly of fearing a 'cage', referring directly to her subservient status within a patriarchal society – she is trapped, and the implications of both her skills with her weapon and her attitude are that she longs to be 'one of the boys', or more aptly, to be allowed to function as an individual rather than be defined and confined by her sex. While she may dress as a medieval princess she does not wish to be that, which may partly explain her developing love for

NOTES:

Representation

Éowyn turns to meet Aragorn's gaze

Aragorn, the sensitive man who notices her plight, and sees her as an individual.

Éowyn's face, in a similar way to Frodo's, is the epitome of despair at various points in the narrative. She is often shown from behind in long shot as a pale silhouette, her hair and gown flowing, against a spectacular backdrop (first at Edoras, also on the eve of battle in **The Return...**). These two uses of Éowyn, as symbol and expression of the human cost of the story, do inevitably use her as object of the look, but perhaps it is more appropriate to see her as a subject of the look – the audience infer the meaning of the shots, and while they may of course admire her beauty and therefore 'to-be-looked-at-ness', her lack of power and frustration within the story could be argued to complicate any implications of sexualisation, but rather be about unhappiness stemming directly from her biology. At times she is subject to the same slow motion look as the other females and Aragorn; for example, as she stands with Gimli, on the way to Helm's

Deep, smiling and watched by Aragorn (so from his point of view, but it is a mutual gaze as she returns it). This indicates once more that the camera lingers on images of either hope or despair, and that Éowyn in particular is symbolic of both.

Before examining more closely her role as transgressor and warrior, we should note that while in the book and in the DVD extended edition of **The Return...** Éowyn abides by both Proppian convention as a princess as well as ultimately accepting her role in a patriarchal society by marrying Faramir, this is omitted from the theatrical version. It may be hinted at but it is not confirmed, therefore in a sense she remains transgressive to the end. However, this is arguably undercut and undermined by the theatrical version in that her most iconic, brave moment in which she slays the Witch King, is totally ignored by all the male characters save a dying Théoden, and as the rest of the men march on to Mordor, Éowyn suddenly disappears from the story entirely. Of course, her heroism has been witnessed by the audience; however, that her defiant act is then glossed over (in the extended version it is made clear just how formidable a foe the Witch King is when he almost kills Gandalf), presumably for the sake of the running time, is, from the perspective of a feminist interpretation, frustrating.

Much has been made, alongside the study of masculinity, of progressive depictions of femininity within the action film. These have occurred mainly in the science fiction genre, with Ripley in the **Alien** films (1979, 1986, 1993, 1997) and Sarah Connor in **Terminator 2** (1991) cited as female characters that

occupy a space where they utilise male characteristics: they fight, wear masculine clothing and are adept with weaponry but do so in order to protect rather than as aggressors, as it were. Although these examples are sadly few, and decades old, increasingly there is an emphasis on the active or dominant female, for example, Trinity in **The Matrix**, and even *Xena* or *Buffy the Vampire Slayer*. Again the issue of displacement appears, with both the science fiction and fantasy genre allowing for more progressive depictions. The main argument against seeing these portrayals as defying Mulvey's argument of passivity are still around their 'to-be-looked-at-ness' – 'When women are portrayed as tough in contemporary film are they being allowed access to a position of empowerment, or are they merely being further fetishised as dangerous sex objects?'[54] In other words are their acts being undermined by the gaze? Although at first this may seem inapplicable to Éowyn, who is not until the end shown as 'tough' and who is seemingly powerless within the patriachal structure, her lack of acceptance embodied in her 'cage' speech, could be seen as her being dangerous – by threatening the order of things. Her act of bravery could thus be seen as exorcising her radical nature in order for her to recognise her 'true' status, that of a passive trophy female. Her image of 'tough' woman is also undermined by her love for Aragorn, which ultimately inspires her to disguise herself, ally herself with another outsider, the hobbit Merry (therefore non-man, so there is an understanding purely based on what they are *not*), and in despair ride to war. Her motives, while initially about her entrapment, develop to be about love, but shift again when she is ultimately rejected by Aragorn.

Through most of the story Éowyn is shown as wanting to fight but being denied the chance. She is instructed in **The Two Towers** by Théoden to lead his people to Helm's Deep, and when she says 'I can fight', he refuses. As they depart for the battle in Gondor, Aragorn finds her hidden sword, thereby questioning

NOTES:

54. Brown, in Innes, *Action Chicks*, 2004

her motives for going, and as her brother Éomer and his friend mock Merry in his attempts to ready himself for bravery, again Éowyn is frustrated – 'why should he not fight?'. What is interesting about Éowyn in relation to other action women is that, unlike Ripley or Sarah Connor in particular, who become more competent and tough because of a direct threat, Éowyn is unhappy from the start. This could be read in response to the threat to those around her, but more progressively as a response to her limited role due to her sex. However, like them, she must ultimately demonstrate her toughness to step up and save her Uncle, when no one else can.

So what does it mean that it is Éowyn who slays the Witch King? It means that given her fight to move beyond her assigned role, given her wish to defend those she loves (therefore act defensively rather than as aggressor, one way in which femininity is 'permitted' to embrace violence) and given her despair, it fulfils all her desires and justifies her wish to move beyond her gender confines. That she is female, and has therefore had to disguise herself to even be in battle, as well as given her unhappiness and sorrow as witnessed by the audience, means her triumph is accentuated. During the enormous battle of Pelennor Fields, this scene is the most personal, as both she and Merry take on the Witch King. Merry's presence, while he aids her by wounding the Witch King, is also interesting in that while he may be a hobbit he is male, yet it is Éowyn who is allowed the principal glory.

Similarly to Aragorn as he decapitates Boromir's killer, Éowyn works as the point of audience identification at this moment, confirming Steve Neale's argument that identification is not bound by gender alone but is far more complex. What is important here is not that she is female, but that she bests a villain of enormous importance within the story, purely by her own actions. No single other main character dispatches such a fearsome foe – Saruman and Sauron for

"I am no man!"

instance, are both dispatched indirectly. It could be argued that the Witch King's Macbeth-esque declaration that no man can kill him reduces Éowyn's act to being about biology. Simply by not being a man she *can* kill him. This paradoxically could be seen to actually enhance her transgression – she is now justified in all her desires not to be 'caged'.

The scene is shot to emphasise her vulnerability – the fell beast, whose head she hacks off, and the Witch King, are both enormous. Both acts demonstrate her physical strength, and of course she is armed with her sword, perceived as phallic and highly masculinised. The mace which the Witch King swings at her is also large, again adding to the suspense in her possible triumph or failure. So their sizes, as well as their weapons, do not match. As discussed in Film Language, disguise is deployed at various points of the story and perhaps most interestingly here. Disguised in male clothing (once more a very Shakespearean device) in armour and a helmet, Éowyn's romantic femininity previously so emphasised by her costume, is here obscured. Éowyn has broken dress codes, and costume is a major signifier of gender and difference. Here it accentuates her transgression into the all-male terrain of battle – she has 'broken symbolic codes of social behaviour'.[55] The disavowal of her gender is redressed when she removes her helmet and reveals herself as a woman, defined by her fairness and blonde hair. Again this is a point of contention – is she by doing this objectifying herself as 'dangerous' female, or is she enhancing the symbolism of the act by performing it as herself? It is arguably the

latter, as the audience already know who she is, therefore the revelation is allowing Éowyn, face exposed, to kill her foe as herself, face to face. That she stabs the Witch King in the face region is also of importance – as discussed previously stabbing weapons are penetrative, and the face is the most expressive and personal part of the body. That her adversary has no face allows her to stab him there with the metaphorical significance of such a 'personal' act not being lost. In relation to the audience's response to her victory as on a par with Aragorn's slaying of Boromir's killer, the two characters can be seen on a certain parallel. While Aragorn's bravery and fearlessness are affirmed again and again, Éowyn's builds to one far more dramatic, climactic moment. This makes her by far the most progressive female in **The Lord of the Rings**, a character who can appropriate and utilise elements of masculinity that are denied to the female elves, who are, in a sense, confined by their to-be-looked-at-ness. This once again highlights the fluidity and mobility of socially constructed gender characteristics acting in conjunction with narcissistic identification. Regardless of sex, the audience will identify with Éowyn at this moment, and should this be seen disparagingly as being Éowyn merely acting as a man, this would once again nullify arguments about her strength stemming from internal demons (similar, but in reverse, to Aragorn's) that come directly from her identity being tied to her gender. Given the traditional nature of the power structures within Middle Earth as well as the overwhelmingly male-centric story, Éowyn is the primary character who allows for a feminist re-interpretation that can position the films alongside the transgressive 'action woman', interestingly here displaced by a past (therefore by a far more binding culture) rather than the more commonly used egalitarian, dystopian/utopian setting of the future. It is also noteworthy that Éowyn is to rule Rohan, on Théoden's instructions, in a deviation from the book where rule passes to Éomer.

NOTES:

55. Tasker, *Spectacular Bodies*, 1993, p150

Film Language
USE OF CAMERA AND EDITING

If one word could be used to describe the use of camera in the films it would be 'movement'. Whether an extreme high angle shot, extreme long shot or circular aerial view, the camera is seldom static but fluid to capture both the constant forward flight of the narrative and the grandeur of Middle Earth.

Peter Jackson's style in shooting the films could be called 'classical' – there are no flashy editing and camera speed techniques evident, for example, in the fight sequences of *Gladiator* (2000). Such a modern aesthetic would look entirely out of place in the mythical world of Middle Earth and Jackson's emphasis on 'realism'. However, this is too simplistic. Jackson's use of the camera in these films is to tell the story in the most effective way, and there are multiple techniques used. Whether whirling aerially or plunging into the depths of Isengard the camera must successfully capture the grandeur and danger of Middle Earth as well as maintain the intimacy of the personal journeys of the different characters. It does this at all times in collaboration with all the other filmic elements, including the soundtrack.

There are many instances of **hand-held camera**. Jackson's camera, at moments of fighting and bloodshed, is often right in the middle of it all. A good example of his deliberate use of the hand-held camera to create immediacy and impact is in *The Fellowship...* within the Mines of Moria. As the Fellowship are trapped by orcs and begin fighting the jerky camera work in close up serves to increase the audience participation. It is used again in *The Two Towers* and *The Return...* at moments of confrontation and conflict and is one style recognisably used throughout the films.

Slow motion is also used regularly, mostly at moments of emotional or dramatic importance, adding to their impact. Examples include when Frodo is stabbed by the cave troll (this coincides with silence or muted sound), as Boromir is mortally wounded and Pippin and Merry are abducted, as Sam almost drowns, at various points in *The Two Towers* relating to Aragorn, when Frodo is stabbed by Shelob and to great effect as Aragorn's army witness the destruction of Mount Doom. This is by no means an exhaustive list, but it indicates the prevalence of the use of the technique at moments of high tension.

The landscape and scale of the films are captured with multiple **aerial shots**, which often place the characters and show locations in extreme long shot. Impossible (CGI) camera shots such as that in *The Fellowship...* when the camera travels all the way from the top of the tower of Orthanc down into the pit where the Urak Hai are being bred also convey the scale. Such shots are visually stunning, as are the extreme zoom outs capturing Saruman's address to his army in *The Two Towers*.

High and **low angled camera** is used, particularly the former, to emphasise either ominous strength (of Sauron in the prologue) or vulnerability (as Sam and Frodo are approached by Gollum for the first time). These shots are in keeping with the emphasis placed on height and its overall narrative function. For example, as Frodo hangs from the precipice inside Mount Doom and as he is carried away by an eagle, we see him from high angle in mortal danger even after the destruction of the Ring.

Gollum approaches the hobbits for the first time

Point of view shots are also widely present. As a rule the subjectivity of the point of view shot is usually used to foster audience identification with a particular character. Here there are many point of view shots, and some are unknown points of view, aimed directly at the audience. An example of how point of view can induce tension and fear is as Frodo enters the lair of Shelob, we see events both from his point of view and from someone else's, suggesting that he is being watched. At other times the point of view is the audience's own, such as in the Mines of Moria sequence with the camera staring into the face of onrushing arrows. The point of view shot is therefore used to offer audience identification for certain key characters and also for audience immersion at moments of action and suspense.

As well as **extreme long shots** being a staple element of the spectacular action, in particular the war film ethic of the wide battle lines and action, **extreme close ups** are also used on particular characters. Frodo, with his increasingly Gollum-like eyes, has, as previously stated, in a sense the face, along with Éowyn, that represents despair.

There are several extreme close ups of people's eyes – from Frodo, Sam and Gollum to Galadriel, Aragorn, Boromir and Gandalf (whose eyes are used as the editing device into his 'death' and 'rebirth'). These occur at times of extreme emotion, danger or importance (Galadriel's eyes are shown in extreme close up in *The Fellowship...* as her mind whispers to Frodo; Aragorn's eyes watch Frodo in Bree and Boromir as he picks up the sword of Isildur at Rivendell). In terms of close ups, some related moments impress. The sequences where Gollum talks to himself (in effect soliloquies that provide the audience subjective access to his thoughts) are cut in such a way that his two personalities are presented in conversation with each other creating each as an entity in its own right. In *The Two Towers* we see Gollum, while Frodo and Sam sleep nearby, agonise with himself over his desire to serve

NOTES:

Frodo, versus his desire to posses the Ring for himself. His 'bad' side, Gollum, and his 'good' side, Sméagol, are separated first by the camera panning from side to side to signify the character shift and then the sequence is edited as if it were a conversation between two characters by using shot-reverse-shot. Gollum's malevolent taunting is shown in a close up (already indicating the dominant power of Gollum over his child-like alter ego) while Sméagol is shown in medium close up. In **The Return...** Jackson uses water as a mirror to create this effect – Gollum, Sméagol's ruthless side, is shown as a reflection in the water, and the editing focuses purely on whoever is talking, which is of course two sides of the same character, but manages to structure the sequences as shot-reverse-shot conversations. It is of note that the trio of Frodo, Sam and Gollum are the characters most often shot in close up, highlighting that theirs is the most emotional storyline with the most personal risks involved (and increasingly aligning Frodo and Gollum).

Sméagol and Gollum 'in conversation'

Where **flashback** is used it is generally accompanied by a voice over or dialogue to contextualise it and for the most part these flashbacks impart information to the viewer as refreshers of key plot points. (The use of flashback in the prologue is discussed under Narrative.) It is also worth looking at the editing for each sequence. The ability film has

to present story events that take place over long periods of time in tightly compressed short sequences allows for much information to be passed to the viewer in a relatively brief amount of screen time. Flashback can be subjective: in **The Return...** flashbacks of both Boromir and Frodo are from the memory of Pippin.

The role of editing is crucial to the successful coherence of the three films, with particularly **The Two Towers** and **The Return...** balancing numerous strands of parallel action. For the most part the films do not draw attention to their construction (and therefore abide by the rules of continuity editing) except where more elegiac or appropriate methods are needed. The use of **cross-cutting** in the films is vital to the narrative as well as to the creation of suspense and tension. Cross-cutting is the way concurrent events and inter-related storylines occurring in different spaces are connected through editing (and is not the same as parallel editing, which shows similar actions occurring at different times).[56] Cross-cutting here ensures that the different groups of characters and their journeys can be shown as occurring simultaneously as well as heightening the tension of both. The different spaces and events shown in cross-cut editing will be expected ultimately to connect to form a resolution of the storylines.

As stated **The Lord of the Rings** films increasingly follow multiple fragmented groups inhabiting different spaces (after the Fellowship breaks at the end of the first film). Occasions when the cross-cutting from one event to another heighten tension include the battle at Helm's Deep, alongside the Ents' decision to fight Saruman, resulting in simultaneous defeats for the enemy. While the resolution connects the events, there is still other action occurring away from this that must be included (Frodo and Sam's journey, for example). It is not until Frodo and Sam's ascent of Mount Doom and Aragorn's arrival with his army outside Mordor that the events all inhabit close geographical space within the

diegesis. Here cross-cutting is used to show the two lines of action and how they finally interlink – as Frodo fights with Gollum, Aragorn is in danger of being killed and the army completely outnumbered. The potential outcome of both situations is disastrous, not only for the quest but also for the characters personally, and the two are edited together to create maximum impact, a technique often used to foster urgency as a film reaches its climactic moment.

This is the most fruitful sequence to analyse in detail in relation to all of the editing and camera techniques outlined. This sequence, the climax of the entire story and upon which the outcome hangs, uses almost every stylistic device mentioned – slow motion, both inside Mount Doom and outside the Black Gate (used extensively in the sequence for dramatic effect); high and low angle shots (Gollum and Frodo in particular and then Sauron's tower as it is finally destroyed); close ups and extreme close ups (again particularly of Sam and Frodo but also Gollum, and the Fellowship characters outside Mordor); fades (to both black and to white, as discussed below); a dissolve, jerky, _verité_-style camera and extreme long shots (as Mordor is destroyed). Along with sound, music and effects the scene is perhaps the most indicative of the range of styles used to best tell the story.

There is a use of non-diegetic text at various points. The opening title to each film, **The Lord of the Rings**, appears before any footage. The typeface is in dulled gold, and is placed on a black screen, implying darkness, the gleaming of the Ring itself and the ancient world in which the story is set. Of note is that the individual film titles do not appear until the end of the prologues, each displayed on top of filmic action – Frodo sitting peacefully in the Shire in **The Fellowship...**, Frodo and Sam advancing to Mordor in **The Two Towers**, and Gandalf and company leaving Fangorn forest in **The Return...**. The effect of this is to unify the films under their umbrella title, and implies that the different sub-

---

NOTES:

56. Hayward, _Key Concepts in Cinema Studies_, 2000, p78

segments are 'chapters' of the larger work. Intertitles are then used only once in the trilogy, at the beginning of **The Fellowship...**, to establish time and place with 'The Shire... 60 years later'. This is the only time there is any written indication of time and place, all others being verbal or visual – although subtitles are occasionally used for dialogue.

The characters use different languages, such as Elvish or Mordor, and are either translated by the use of subtitles, by alternating between the particular language and English, or by English replacing the 'foreign' language. The latter is used during the prologue to the first film, where Cate Blanchett's voice is heard whispering in Elvish over a black screen, only to then start her voice over in English. Many of the characters are multi-lingual, allowing for some conversations to be held between certain characters and not understood by those around them, a device used particularly between Legolas and Aragorn that creates a hierarchy of knowledge within the diegesis. The conversations between these two and between Aragorn and Arwen oscillate between Elvish (with subtitles) and English, and successfully achieve a straight-forward transition between the two.

In summary, the use of camera and editing alone provide ample material for considerable study of the films, to depict either the harsh realism required at one end of the scale (in the case of battle sequences and hand-held camera) as well as the magical nature of Middle Earth at the other, with spectacle and narrative being best served at all times. The use of both is heavily associated with sound and soundtrack.

SOUND AND SOUNDTRACK

Without soundtracks to render artificial creations and effects 'real', much of the use of digital technology would be ineffective within contemporary cinema. It is part of the suspension of disbelief by audiences – not only do the eyes have to be convinced, so too do the ears. Despite this, sound is often marginalised when analysing film texts, despite its power both as signifier of meaning within narratives and its use of music to foster emotions and guide the viewer in moments of dramatic tension, anticipation, sadness and joy.

Sound on film can be divided into two basic categories: **diegetic** and **non-diegetic**. Diegetic means everything within the story world that in theory the characters can hear (sounds of battle, animal cries, dialogue, etc.), and non-diegetic is everything that the audience hears outside the world of the story (for example, music score and voice overs). Both work together to offer an all-round sensory experience.

In terms of effects, with many of the creatures and sequences of **The Lord of the Rings** being artificially constructed, sounds had to be created that would bring them to life, and the DVDs are filled with information about the lengths to which sound designers went to ensure authenticity (**The Two Towers** extended DVD in particular offers a very useful look at the Helm's Deep sequence with the different sound effects subdivided into eight tracks). For example, the sounds of arrows being fired and penetrating bodies were recorded in the open air to ensure it matched the scenes.

There are other times when sound is explicitly used to generate a sense of 'otherness', for example, during the moments when Frodo wears the Ring and is transported into another dimension. The sound used in these sequences, along with the effects, is a method of presenting these as experiences both for Frodo and for the audience, often accompanied by point of view or slow motion camera. Eerie sounds and whispers are also used to form the personality and power of the Ring, with Frodo becoming increasingly at its mercy (for example, in **The Two Towers** as he and Sam are taken to Gondor and he almost surrenders the Ring to a Ringwraith).

Sound is also used in editing to bridge scenes, a good example of this being in **The Two Towers**, immediately after Frodo and Sam have captured Gollum at night, when his wailing carries across to the following scene during the day. The muting of sound and music is also a device used at pivotal points. Mostly used in combination with slow motion camera, it is a highly effective means of creating suspense for the audience and tends to be used in particularly grave situations. There are examples in each film: in **The Fellowship...** as Frodo is speared by the cave troll in the Mines of Moria and as Boromir is wounded (with music and muted sound playing a key part in his subsequent death and Merry and Pippin's capture); in **The Two Towers** as Aragorn tumbles from the cliff and as Haldir (the leader of the elf army) is killed at Helm's Deep; in **The Return...** as Théoden is attacked by the Witch King and as Frodo is stabbed by Shelob. These moments of silence or muted sound are often at extreme odds with the action surrounding them (usually the chaos of battle) and therefore highly effective in directing the audience to focus on the gravity of one sole incident, which will usually have serious dramatic consequences.

The Lord of the Rings films have a magnificently orchestral score, symphonic and operatic in scale and ambition and scope, in keeping with the films and their epic nature. Film music is increasingly at the forefront of popular new classical music and extends audiences additional public appeal (for example, the success of **Titanic** (1997) was mirrored by an incredibly popular musical score). The music was composed by Howard Shore whose list of film scores is staggeringly diverse, having scored the majority of David Cronenberg's films, as well as **Se7en** (1995), **High Fidelity** (2000) and **The Silence of the Lambs**. Interestingly, it seems the celebrity status awarded film score composers resembles auteurism (far more so than, say, cinematography).

NOTES:

Once again Jackson's 'hands on' cottage industry approach to film-making meant he worked with Shore on areas of the score and his partner Fran Walsh devised both themes and lyrics for the songs at the end of each film.

As with the other filmic elements (effects, costume, mise-en-scène, etc.), music plays a vital role in creating and maintaining the feel of Middle Earth as believable yet 'otherworldly'. More complexly, music is used to differentiate between its numerous, diverse locations and characters as well as create emotional resonance with the audience. One of film music's most pivotal roles in film is to 'channel a certain field of readings… to foster emotional identification'.[57] This is true no matter what the genre. With **The Lord of the Rings**, the scale of the musical score had to be as large and expansive as the visuals. It had to work to demonstrate the cultures, as well as the plight, of Middle Earth. It also had to work on a more intimate level and emphasise the emotional/spiritual journeys undertaken by many of the characters. As with special effects, there are innumerable musical elements that could be analysed; here a selection of instances will be used as examples of the overall tone and impact of the musical score.

One way to approach the music of the films is to look at how themes are used for different locations and spheres of action. Much of the thematic resonance of certain places is maintained by the music, which can be re-introduced to symbolise the emotion or action associated with that particular place. A prime example of this is the music that represents the Shire. The Shire works as the haven and 'home' for the entire story. A simple melody that plays as Frodo is seen for the first time in **The Fellowship...** (played on the clarinet), is reintroduced at times as Frodo and Sam reminisce about the Shire, most movingly as the two remember the Shire on their final ascent of Mount Doom. Another example is how the theme of the Fellowship develops until it is fully formed as the party leave Rivendell and is heard in its last version as Frodo stands alone at the end of the film, poised to embark on his quest, and thus break the Fellowship.

In keeping with the ancient nature of Middle Earth a whole range of instruments and orchestrations are used. There is an emphasis on choral music and it appears in a diverse range of forms, from a boys' choir, huge male voice choir to solo voices (different ones chosen to represent different places and storylines). For the Elven havens such as Rivendell and Lothlórien the voices create a suitably unearthly ambience (with the case of Rivendell the theme then had to incorporate the love story between Arwen and Aragorn), while for the Ringwraiths far more aggressive use is made of voices in a minor key. These themes can again reappear at different points of the narrative (for example, as the elves arrive at Helm's Deep or as Galadriel reaches out to Frodo in Shelob's lair) maintaining continuity and great command over the coherence of the story. Notably the use of the young male voice is particularly effective at the end of **The Fellowship...**, in choir form as the Ents march on Isengard in **The Two Towers**, and as Gollum finally possesses the Ring while falling to his death in **The Return...**.

Themes are given to races and cultures, with Rohan's Viking-esque rustic culture represented by the lone violin (associated with Celtic and folk music) or trumpets, with Eastern instruments used and with Gondor's theme played first on the French horn. Likewise Isengard, Saruman and the Urak Hai are accompanied by heavy, angry, metallic chords and low brass while shots of Mordor and Sauron are to a more frantic, high pitched but still minor musical motif. In places of heightened drama or emotion in the films there is a dense use of music and sound, for example, during the battle sequences when the grandeur and expanse of the visuals must be audibly matched. There are also themes where music denotes the melodramatic moments of the story, in particular those between Arwen and Aragorn, Sam and Frodo. The use of motifs relates to the overall score yet is more 'intimate' and personal.

Although the vast majority of the music in the films is non-diegetic, there are moments in which song is used. These add another layer of 'history' to Middle Earth (all ancient cultures not only have myth but song). Pippin's song, sung to Denethor in **The Return...**, is an interesting use of diegetic sound to foster emotion. As he sings the scene shows Faramir, Denethor's son, riding to almost certain death, as the Steward himself eats bloody meats (the crunching of bones accentuated). As at many other times in the films, the combination of editing, camera, sound and music heighten dramatic and atmospheric effect.

The end credits of each film are also accompanied by a theme song that relates to the thematic music of the particular film and is clearly meant to be both emblematic of the film and more modern (therefore a potential 'tie-in' song) often sung by a familiar vocalist. The first is sung by Enya, the second by Icelandic singer Emiliana Torrini (whose voice remarkably resembles Bjork's, who was allegedly approached several times to sing the track) and finally Annie Lennox. One of their most noteworthy aspects of all the female voices is how they follow on from the final musical themes of each film (for example, Gollum's Song in **The Two Towers** which is based on the music playing at the close of action in the film, and Into the West for **The Return...**, emblematic of the music that accompanies Frodo's departure). The latter is arguably a swansong not only for Frodo but the entire story and all three films.

NOTES:

57. Gorbman, In Church-Gibson and Hill, *The Oxford Guide to Film Studies*, 1998

Film Language

LOCATIONS/ SETTING

Locations and settings are pivotally interlinked with the narrative and themes of **The Lord of the Rings**. Not only is the constant narrative drive forwards epitomised and emphasised by the physical movement of the characters from place to place given its simple quest narrative, the journey undertaken must present multiple obstacles and hardships. Often these come in the form of the locations.

This forward movement provides a near-constant variety of cinematic spectacle for the audience. 'Locations can not only be recognised and help us to place the characters within a film, but can also through the film itself create their own space and meaning.'[58] Space here constructs both the film's internal diegetic and narrative logic, and offers the spectatorial pleasures of visual engagement that have come to be expected from the saturation release, event film. The viewer is presented with a multitude of breathtakingly cinematic views of vast plains, eerie woodlands, ominous mountains, festering marshes, glaciers, walls of rock, cavernous underground mines, illuminated tree-top dwellings, ethereal Elven havens… the list could go on.

As discussed in Narrative, location sits at the heart of the story – Frodo cannot destroy the Ring anywhere other than in the heart of Mordor, and even more specifically inside Mount Doom (the name itself obviously portentous). Immediately the two extremes of the story – the peace-loving, snug and pastoral Shire (established following the prologue in **The Fellowship…**) stands in juxtaposition to the blackened, fiery Mordor (shown in the prologue), and it is these two geographical/metaphorical extremes that book-end all the places in between. But more fundamental than this is the use of **displacement**.

The fantasy genre, like science fiction, tends to transport culturally familiar themes and stories to distant settings. Often this is interpreted as a way for contemporaneous anxieties to be played out and discussed in the relative 'safety' of the unfamiliar, or more particularly relevant here, 'to enable pleasure in the escapism of fantasy and entertainment – the all-enveloping immersion in another world'.[59] This displacement is achieved by **The Lord of the Rings** in many ways in its mise-en-scène, use of music, costume, weaponry (in other words all the components work towards creating a fully immersive experience by striving for diegetic 'realism'). But more essentially this detachment is achieved by its use of setting in terms of geography and time. The world of Middle Earth is remote from ours through its very name and the names of all the places within it in addition to their appearance, and the story appears to be set in an ancient past. This can therefore allow us to immerse ourselves in the wonder of a world that is familiar enough yet distanced from us, and indulge in the escapist pleasures that it offers. The universal themes in the story, of good versus evil, are familiar, as are the characterisations, and by using societies that are culturally familiar, such as city dwellings and monarchies, this otherness versus familiarity is also evident in the film's locations.

For cinema-goers, regardless of the 'otherness' of the story of Middle Earth, the actual landscapes shown are also unfamiliar. The oft-filmed USA is nowhere to be seen, having been replaced by a much less familiar landscape. The actual location of the production was New Zealand (Jackson's home), a country of two small islands with diverse terrains, from glaciers to rainforests, fjords to snow-capped mountain ranges. This landscape is used as the basis for Middle Earth. However, given the impact of digital manipulation on each film (not merely the spectacular effects but 'digital grading' as looked at under Special Effects, whereby colours and shades are enhanced), it is

deliberately an 'other' world. It looks something like ours, but is different enough to create distance.

So, setting and locations are foregrounded in the films, both in terms of narrative necessity and audience experience. One common denominator connects all the diverse locations used within the films – they are all *vast*. The sheer size and scale of Middle Earth is constantly changing but always dramatic. The positioning of characters in such spaces serves to emphasise certain characteristics. For example the hobbits living in the Shire have physically small homes that create some amusement at the opening of **The Fellowship…** for Gandalf, but once they are out of their own habitat their diminutive stature in contrast to the enormity of Middle Earth serves to emphasise their vulnerability. Similarly the dwellings of the elves at Rivendell and Lothlórien with their dream-like soft focus cascading waterfall or illuminated tree top havens visually code these places as idylls. They provide some of the few moments of respite in the narrative of the films.

Set against these havens are the dangerous places of Middle Earth, where evil seems to actually 'live'. Mordor and the formerly rural Isengard become the industrial wastelands that contrast with the beauty of the rest of Middle Earth. Mordor's blackened landscape and fiery mountain are often visible to the characters from the Fellowship in the distance, the red glowing just above the dark mountains that are often shown on the horizon. These glances forward serve to keep that place firmly established as the geographical goal of the story, but also to inspire dread.

The films are book-ended with maps of Middle Earth, providing some sense of the geography of the place. The first location introduced after the prologue which establishes history, the overall space of Middle Earth, Mordor and Sauron/Ring, is the Shire. Its function is not only to create a safe haven,

NOTES:

58. Nelmes, *An Introduction to Film Studies 3rd Ed*, 2003, p65
59. Scarratt, E, *Science Fiction Film: A Teacher's Guide*, 2001, p74

a rural idyll for the peace-loving peasant hobbit folk (upon whose incorruptibility the entire fate of Middle Earth lies), it serves as the nostalgic 'home' for the story. Once a threat is introduced to the Shire in the shape of the Black Riders, this safety is undermined. It also marks the contrast between the two – one shot in *The Fellowship...* uses clever mise-en-scène to show the Shire landscape with an ominous silhouette of a Black Rider appearing in the foreground. It is archetypally English, as indicated by its name and the pastoral lifestyle of its inhabitants. It is talked of with melancholy and nostalgia by Sam and Frodo in times of hardship. Its green pastures and blue skies are increasingly literally a world away from their dark and inhospitable surroundings as they journey towards Mordor.

The journey of the four hobbits once they leave the Shire becomes more dangerous, and as they arrive at the village of Bree, mise-en-scène and over-sized props are used to signify that the hobbits don't belong. Breaking down the locations within the film it becomes clear that rarely do the characters enter or cross the same terrain twice. In *The Fellowship...* it is the sole group that we follow, alongside parallel action in Isengard. But, as discussed, in the later films there are different storylines occurring at the same time in entirely different locations. Nevertheless the groups of characters all move forward to new geographical terrain almost constantly. Each of these journeys must have its own forward-moving coherence, and often it is characters within the films who explain where they are (Aragorn, for instance, as they reach Rohan, or Gimli as they stand outside Fangorn Forest). Each location brings further complication to the narrative, resulting in spectacular visual set-pieces caused by a new disequilibrium. This creates an over-arching theme that no place is actually safe. In *The Fellowship...* the hobbits believe they will be safe in Bree, but are not. Gandalf rides to Isengard believing it to be the haven of the wise Saruman, but it then becomes his prison. The Mines of Moria

The Shire and Mount Doom stand as polarised good/evil locations

and even the water outside them have their own perils. This movement from one location only to flee to another is of course integral to a chase narrative that offers us first the Black Riders then the Urak Hai as the 'chasers', and these regular obstacles are how the journey to fulfil the quest becomes not just physically dangerous but metaphorically so.

No matter whether depicting interior or exterior locations there is an emphasis on height. In *The Fellowship...* alone, Gandalf is held captive on the top of Orthanc (at Isengard), Weathertop (where Frodo is stabbed) is a set high up on the top of a mountain, Rivendell sits high up in a valley, Lothlórien is housed within an immensely tall

NOTES:

Film Language

forest, and the Mines of Moria are replete with a vast, cathedral-like hall with huge pillars (covered in intricate Elvish carvings), so impressive that even the characters within the story stop to marvel at them just as we do. This is also true of the Argonath (huge stone carvings of Gondor's past Kings). This traversing of different locations also allows for different means of transport, again maintaining diversity (as well as at times touching on generic codes, for example, the use of the horse over vast plains is synonymous with the Western). It is notable that apart from the use of a boat to escape, Frodo and Sam are the only two characters who walk barefoot all the way to their destination.

Again heights are important within the second film. Locations in *The Two Towers* are less linear than the first film. The splintered Fellowship each follow different paths. As this is in a sense the second act in the story, and therefore in a virtually constant state of disequilibrium there is little respite offered by any of the locations. There is absolutely none offered to Frodo and Sam, their journey becoming more perilous across different terrain, the rocky journey through Emyn Muil giving way to the expansive and terrifying Dead Marshes and the industrial slurry outside the Black Gate of Mordor. Even moments of light relief (for example, Sméagol and Sam's argument over food) are quickly followed by dramatic turns. It is the remainder of the Fellowship who introduce new characters by entering new lands, for example, Rohan and Fangorn Forest. All of these come with height references or use of heights for dramatic purpose. For example, Frodo, Sam and Gollum are tracked by a swooping Fell Beast across the Dead Marshes, Sam tumbles down the rock slurry outside the Black Gate, as Frodo watches an endangered Gollum as he swims below in a 'forbidden pool', and Frodo stands trance-like high on the ramparts in Gondor, holding the Ring out to a Black Rider. The other characters also deal with heights – Pippin and Merry are scooped up

Helm's Deep

and carried by the Ent, Treebeard, while the remainder of the Fellowship travel to the hilltop dwelling of Edoras in Rohan and then on to Helm's Deep, whose high walls form the basis of many of the spectacular fighting scenes in the battle sequence.

Additionally there is the dramatic plunge and mountaintop fight of Gandalf with the Balrog (Gandalf's 'death' is shown by a CGI shot of the universe, the only extra-diegetic shot not showing Middle Earth in the entire three films). Aragorn falls from a cliff face, and as Gandalf finally arrives with the Rohirrim at Helm's Deep they charge down a near-vertical mountainside. In *The Return...* once more the drama and danger of events are exemplified by heights to an even greater degree. Frodo and Sam's locations for the third film become smaller destinations around and within Mordor, each becoming more perilous until the climactic scene inside Mount Doom. Their physical journey mirrors the danger they face from Gollum – they increasingly become at risk from great heights the nearer they draw to their destination. Their ascent into Mordor up near-sheer cliff-face stairs is exploited as they are shot from above, highlighting their vulnerability. The audience also know, from Gollum's monologue at the end of *The Two Towers*, to anticipate something unsavoury if and when they reach the top. At the final stage of their journey again they must face heights – a gruelling climb to the top of Mount Doom, which seems nearly beyond them, again working to make their task even more difficult and their success even more unlikely.

The world of 'men' is based around two specific locations, Rohan and Gondor. Locations, alongside costume, music and props, signify difference. For example, the people of Rohan live in wood and thatched houses, the royal mountaintop of Edoras is fortified and constructed from wood. The halls of their city are intricately decorated with symbols of their culture (horses), and this style of living gives them as a people a Viking-esque identity. Conversely Gondor, with its ancient cliff-side marble white city of Minas Tirith, is an entirely different civilisation more easily identifiable for us as Roman. Towards the end of *The Return...* as Aragorn is crowned and people kneel before the hobbits, the camera moves away from Minas Tirith, emphasising its height, also signifying the end of the quest.

Parallel action in different locations also heightens tension and this is increasingly the case in the climactic film. As Aragorn takes the Paths of the Dead (often shot from above) the battle is raging and once almost won a new army appears to defeat the Rohirrim. Once finally won, all the characters assemble outside the Black Gate, drawing them geographically closer to the storyline occurring inside Mordor with Frodo and Sam. The reuniting of the Fellowship and the restoration of Aragorn to the throne then occur in Minas Tirith, before the film then follows only the hobbits as they journey home. It is only the hobbits that have a place to return to. All the other principal characters are strangely homeless – a displaced King who was a Ranger, now 'home' for the first time; an elf and a dwarf whose backgrounds are never fully established, and Gandalf, again who seems to move from place to place and has no true home (which may in part explain his love for the hobbit life and the Shire). They meet and ally themselves with different places and races. It is therefore narratively appropriate that given the Shire is the location most firmly established within the first film as the safe idyll, once equilibrium is restored it is where our heroes return to. It must be noted that in the books the Shire has

NOTES:

been ravaged and scoured by Saruman and Wormtongue on the hobbits' return. In the films, it is portrayed as being exactly the same as when they left, to emphasise the changes that have occurred within the characters themselves. Which leads to the final destinations. While the other three hobbits can re-establish their lives within the Shire, Frodo cannot. The final journey of the elves, Bilbo, Gandalf and Frodo can be seen in different ways. As they sail off into a serene sunset, their actual destination is left deliberately unclear, except that it is so far away (in another dimension, i.e. heaven?) that they are never to return.

What is not made clear is what all these places *are*. In the cases of Gondor and Rohan they are Kingdoms, places of men. Likewise Rivendell and Lothlórien are Elven havens. Mordor is described as the 'land of Mordor' by Gandalf, but what is the Shire? By implication of name it is a county. Much of the geography of the story is offered by maps, and the names given for the place by the characters within the diegetic world. These seem to offer enough information to the viewer not to question the various set-ups of these places, and one word in particular is noticeable by omission – the word 'country' is not used, creating perhaps a fantastical world with fewer boundaries and divisions than our own.

COSTUME

Costume can be vitally important in establishing verisimilitude, particularly in terms of genre where it can work as generic iconography and create 'authenticity', here fundamental to the creation of Middle Earth as a credible place. The types of costume on display in *The Lord of the Rings* mobilise the cultural histories of various ancient civilisations, from Vikings to Romans, Saxons and medieval times and so on. Along with other elements of mise-en-scène the films' accompanying DVD 'making of'

documentaries emphasise the painstaking work that went into creating the costumes – indicating that spectacular costumes are appealing in their own right. For many genres costume is key to their formal qualities – the suits and tommyguns of the gangster genre or the cowboy outfits and hats of the Western are iconic visual shorthand. In terms of *The Lord of the Rings* the emphasis is on diegetic coherence and the costumes therefore function to heighten the realism of setting rather than offer any immediate generic similarity.

The story of *The Lord of the Rings* occurs within a pre-technological world. Any notion of 'fashion' seems entirely absent in the sense that the world portrayed is ancient (fashion connoting modernity). The costumes used are vital in reaffirming this 'otherworldliness' yet must bear some relevance to our cultural codes in order to work on a level of familiarity. This is where the use of costume becomes complex, in how it can aid the setting or time period of a film but also work on the level of identification for the audience.

'Costume plays a key role in the construction of gender codes and expectations.'[60] This is certainly the case in *The Lord of the Rings* where the differences between male and female as well as race are marked by costume. The male costumes are largely functional in their sensibility, being unconcerned with fashion. The costumes vary, however the fabrics and designs all attempt to maintain the credibility of the diegetic world. The female costumes, looked at in more detail later, are by contrast lavish and romantic. Let us firstly look at the presentation of the races and principal characters.

Firstly, in terms of appearance, with the exception of the hobbits and the elves, the men of *The Lord of the Rings* are all bearded, and all of them to some degree have long hair. This emphasises the ancient world as well as using their biological sex as a defining characteristic of gender difference. Kings here can have long hair (e.g. Théoden) but are

elevated above those around them by ornate costume. Bright colours are almost totally absent in all the costumes unless they clothe royalty. The civilised, hierarchical but functional nature of life in Middle Earth is replicated in the costuming and picks up on thematic issues of the natural; not only must the colours seem so but also the types of fabric. The majority of the male costumes are in earthy, organic colours – greens, browns, greys – and fabrics, like suede, leather, velvet and coarse weave. Boromir is one of the few characters to wear both black and red (his costume works to highlight his status that is then undermined by Aragorn's true identity and moral strength), and Arwen wears blue velvet, but apart from these the costumes are for the most part similar in colour to their natural surroundings.

Character function is also emphasised by costume, perhaps most obviously in the character of Gandalf. Not only does he state almost immediately upon introduction that he is a wizard, all his attire works to indicate this too. It is also used to signify his transformation. As Gandalf the Grey he wears a pointy wizard's hat, has long unruly greying hair and a similarly straggly beard. His robes are grey and his staff is wooden with a knarled tip. His modest appearance belies his enormous power and strength. Upon his reappearance in *The Two Towers* he is transformed. Blinding light, and the use of the voice of Saruman gradually morphing into Gandalf's, announce him as Gandalf the White, with sleek white hair and beard, no hat, pristine white robes and accompanying white staff. He is now also accompanied by an all-powerful white horse. This use of white, to indicate power and majesty, is an interesting about-turn after the use of white to symbolise the evil hand of Saruman. This implies the elevation of Gandalf's powers as matching those of Saruman, which is shown to be the case as he exorcises King Théoden after revealing himself in his new, more powerful, incarnation.

NOTES:

60. Street, *Costume and Cinema*, 2001, p3

Film Language

Gandalf's costume change emphasises his transformation

Disguise and transformation through costume are also used elsewhere. Gandalf, on returning in **The Two Towers**, disguises himself as Gandalf the Grey to enter Théoden's realm, Frodo and Sam wear orc armour to approach Mount Doom and, of course, Aragorn is a king in disguise, dressed as a Ranger. In terms of character function, therefore, Aragorn is not dressed as he should be – his outfit as a Ranger is not the outfit of a king, and when he is revealed as such at the council meeting in Rivendell, it is a surprise. He wears muted colours (contrasting with the grandeur of the subordinate Boromir's attire) and textures such as leather and suede when he journeys, then wearing more luscious velvets during breaks in the journey (e.g. at Rivendell). He is another character whose transformation is mirrored by his costume. As he leads the armies to the outside of Mordor and the Black Gate he does this in the attire of Gondor for the first time, his ascension to the throne unofficially completed by summoning the cursed Dead Army from the Paths of the Dead. Ultimately he is crowned King, his transformation complete, now in his 'rightful' costume.

The most trangressive use of costume and disguise is by Éowyn, who disguises herself in masculine battle dress only to reveal herself as a woman as she slays the Witch King. Symbolically this lends her masculine traits, temporarily masking her femininity. Costume can also therefore symbolise change, here in relation to Éowyn, or in the preparation for the battle at Helm's Deep, as the changing into battle armour works to build tension and anticipation as well as being suggestive of the horror of war.

Differences between races are also personified both by costume and appearance. For example, the people of Rohan are blonde (both the peasant folk and the royals, Théoden, Éowyn and Éomer), wearing mainly greens and browns. Their emblem of the horse is shown on their flags, and their habitat is organic and Viking-esque. By contrast the kingdom of Gondor is differentiated in several ways. Firstly, there is the difference in their living styles (Roman-esque living in the grandiose, tall marble city of Minas Tirith), inferring differences in their civilisations. As people they are given different costumes, wearing blacks and greys (which contrast against the white backgrounds). Their hair is black or at least very dark, and the women wear headscarves, which along with covering their hair (i.e. one of their potentially most feminine

characteristics) also carries religious connotations. There are then their differing forms of battle dress – armour, chain mail, helmets of different colour. This enables the recognition of lots of digital extras used in the expansive battle scenes by their costume alone.

It is not just 'men' whose costume signifies race and background. The dwarves are dressed in hefty metal armour; conversely the deftness of Legolas and the elves is accentuated in their sleek and elegant outfits (the golden shine and shape of which sets them apart from the people of Rohan during the battle of Helm's Deep). Likewise the hobbits are a race whose simple peasant lifestyle is established very early on in the first film not only through their habitat but through their dress. That they have large, hairy feet differentiates them from humans, with this earthiness emphasised further by their short trousers and unshod feet. They also wear braces over shirts and English-style waistcoats. Items of costume are not purely decorative in the three films, they can bear a direct relation to and influence the narrative. For example, both Bilbo and Frodo's waistcoats feature a pocket that can store the Ring. Incidentally another article of clothing of practical use is the Elven cloaks which the entire Fellowship wear upon departing from Lothlórien. Not only do they conceal Frodo and Sam outside the Black Gate in Mordor, the brooch which ties them is deliberately dropped by Merry as they are taken by the Urak Hai.

The material used for the Baggins' clothing is velvet, connoting on some level wealth. Bilbo wears a striking red waistcoat at the opening of **The Fellowship...**, and as Frodo and Sam set off to leave the Shire Frodo is wearing a brown velvet waistcoat and jacket. The other two hobbits they encounter, Pippin and Merry, also wear waistcoats, and it is noticeable that only Sam does not. The inter-class friendship between the two is in part illustrated by the costume differences (as well as Sam's West Country accent in comparison to Frodo's Queen's English). As they continue on their

NOTES:

journey and their differences even out, their appearance also becomes more similar, both wearing elven cloaks, and the dirtiness of their clothes diminishes Frodo's more upper-class trappings to those of the purely functional. Both are then pitched against the creature of Gollum.

Gollum's appearance says much about his character. He is physically pathetic. Near naked with only a tiny, dirty loincloth, he is a creature whose appearance symbolises that he has nothing. No possessions, no dignity, he is an outcast. His desire for the Ring is so strong that it is all-consuming, and he has time or thoughts for nothing else. He moves like a beast, on all fours, and never stands upright. Along with his volatile dual personality this sets Gollum apart from all the other characters. It also means his movements can be very specific to his personality and his status which when he is captured by Frodo and Sam becomes one of almost a pet, fetching food and being eager to please.

Gollum's 'costume' and appearance signifies the all-consuming power of the Ring

In the prologue to **The Return...** we see Gollum in his original form as Sméagol, a hobbit-like creature. We witness his horrifying transformation into the cursed and lonely murderer Gollum, an addict and slave to the Ring. His costume here mirrors almost exactly that of the hobbits, and furthers the parallels between Gollum and Frodo should Frodo be seduced by the Ring. This parallel is rendered physical in the increasing similarity between the haunted, watery blue eyes of Gollum and those of Frodo as the Ring becomes a heavier burden.

As touched on in Representation, the prominent female characters wear by far the most flamboyant and colourful costumes. The main female characters, Éowyn, Arwen and Galadriel, all wear princess-like, medieval dresses that touch the ground and have long, flared sleeves. They all also have very long, flowing hair (either very blonde, in the case of Galadriel and Éowyn, or very dark, as with Arwen). This style again reinforces the ancient setting, their hair reminiscent of fairy tales such as Rapunzel. Their costumes therefore move, and stand out, far more than those worn by the male characters.

While not apparently fashionable, each of the female characters is in possession of a traditionally female characteristic that is still overwhelmingly present in our society – they are all beautiful. Their hair, costume and faces all combine to reinforce a very feminine idea of beauty, with two of the three being immortal and therefore impervious to the effects of time.

These costumes are also, of course, entirely impractical for anything like the fighting and battles undertaken by the male characters. In terms of the impact of costume on narrative, two of the main female characters, Galadriel and Arwen, are elves, not human, and are thus imbued with a sense of grace and ephemeral beauty. It is Éowyn who transgresses her role and her disguise as a soldier in **The Return...** is symbolic of this (as discussed in Representation).

There is a heavy emphasis on the uses of cloaks and capes. As well as the cloaks of Lothlórien many of the characters are shown either hooded

Traditional notions of 'fairy tale' femininity are to the fore

or concealed. Aragorn is hooded at Bree until he reveals himself as the hobbits' protector. Faramir is also introduced hooded. Of course the Black Riders are hooded, as are at various points Arwen, Galadriel and the hobbits. One particular moment where Arwen's capes are used to create a powerful image is in **The Return...**. After returning to Rivendell, having seen a vision of her future son with Aragorn, she stands over Isildur's broken sword. Her face is shown within her hood/shroud and the angle at which she holds her head and her expression are reminiscent of depictions of the Madonna throughout art history (as is the statue of Aragorn's mother, shown in the extended DVD version of **The Fellowship...**). In addition to hoods other headwear can be used, such as helmets, which can also serve as narrative devices, their donning indicating an imminent battle sequence. It is worth noting that Aragorn does not wear any helmets, and neither do Legolas or Gandalf (and Gimli wears his almost

NOTES:

constantly) making these central characters instantly recognisable in the battle sequences, and keeping them as the emotional focus of identification for the scenes.

The use of costume as a shorthand to connote character function is nowhere more evident than in the presentation of the evil characters. There are too many characters to count in the trilogy, and many of these are the hundreds of digitally created characters used in the sweeping battle scenes – the 10,000 Urak Hai sent to attack Helm's Deep in **The Two Towers**, the countless orcs and men used in the Battle of Pelennor Fields in **The Return....**. Attire in these instances becomes vital – 'minor characters are often primarily identified on the basis of costume'.[61] In relation to the Urak Hai they have been bred by Saruman (therefore unnaturally created) and are terrifying for their utter lack of fear and compassion, their pure hatred and lust for carnage. For the most part the Urak Hai are primal, base and bestial. These traits are emphasised in their physicality.

They are immensely large and strong, with muscular legs and arms. They notably and symbolically only wear armour on their fronts, indicating that they will never retreat. Their weapons (see also Weaponry and Props) are hacking, one-sided blades (in other words not suitable for graceful fencing, only slicing and cutting) or spears, none of them shiny or well-crafted but functional.

The animalistic nature of the Urak Hai is heightened by costume in their style of helmet. In **The Two Towers**, as an army of 10,000 Urak Hai converge on Helm's Deep, we see only their mouths and their sharp, animal teeth as they growl and roar in anticipation. No eyes, so no personal features.

While physical strength is of prime importance in the use of costume and appearance for the Urak Hai, the villains introduced earlier who are formidable in a

different way are the Black Riders. They are most threatening in **The Fellowship...** As the other films progress they are still a pervasive threat (swooping over the Dead Marshes, hovering over Gondor, attacking retreating soldiers, etc.). However, it is in the first film that they are at their most powerful. As they arrive in the Shire they are mainly shot in silhouette and in shadow, starkly contrasting with the peaceful landscape. Their costume and the way they are shot have an important purpose. They are wearing black, their hooded costume masking their heads, rendering them faceless and hollow. Only when Frodo puts on the Ring at Weathertop in **The Fellowship...** do we see them in their 'true' state, as white, ghostly Kings with tortured faces. The remainder of the time they are in black, with black horses. In terms of framing the camera often focuses on either their feet or their hands. Their feet, complete with pointed metal spikes on their shoes, are shown in accompaniment to the hooves of their huge black horses. Their hands are shown in armour, again with jagged metal spikes, and insects fall from their gowns. Due to their 'undead' state, as characters they are already fearsome, it being seemingly impossible that they can be killed. Their appearance in silhouette, in the dark, backlit by misty moonlight, renders them even more terrifying.

WEAPONRY AND PROPS

Props and weapons, as part of the overall mise-en-scène of a film, can provide information about both genre and characters. The focus on particular props can convey significance to the story[62] and can also embody meaning about the characters. In keeping with the use of dress to emphasise the ancient world, **The Lord of the Rings** includes battles and fights where modern technology, at least within the guise of the weaponry of the story, has no place. There are no guns here (so often pervasive within

action cinema), and weaponry is ancient, from heavy Arthurian swords to the light arrows of the elves. All the weapons are in some way primitive. The use of psychoanalytical theory when looking at such weapons highlights the penetrative nature of not just swords but the majority of ancient weaponry, including spears, axes, arrows and daggers.

Psychoanalytically, the swords can represent the phallus. That the characters of 'men' wield larger swords indicates in Freudian terms their dominant status (providing a point of identification for the males in the audience) while the females could represent 'lack'. However, this argument is problematised in the films, because both Arwen and particularly Éowyn gain access to the male terrain of swords and wield them with power and competence. They are not, as psychoanalytical theory would have it, 'lacking'.

The human men wield the largest swords of all the characters. The hobbits are each offered swords by Aragorn as they camp on Weathertop in **The Fellowship...**, and it is noticeable that these swords are in keeping with the size of the hobbits. One of Frodo's magical gifts includes a sword (Sting) that glows as orcs approach, again of a similar size but also denoting Frodo as the more vitally important and better-equipped (and more virile?) hobbit of the quartet.

This 'coding' of the characters according to their weapons acts as a pattern of differentiation not just for individuals but also for races, alongside costume. For instance, Gimli's belligerent, stubborn nature and height as a dwarf mean an axe is his suitable weapon, just as the grace of the slight and nimble Legolas means his strength lies in the use of a sleek, slender bow and arrow. The Urak Hai carry noticeably savage and primitive weapons. The use of battle weaponry also has narrative pertinence, for example with regard to Boromir's shield or horn, as evidence of his whereabouts.

NOTES:

61. Nelmes, *An Introduction to Film Studies 3rd Ed*, 2003, p67
62. ibid., p66

The use of explosives is largely greeted with disbelief. Saruman's army carry with them two bombs, with an Olympian-esque Urak Hai responsible for lighting the fuses at Helm's Deep in *The Two Towers*. This is the turning point in the battle, where Théoden, previously believing his fortress to be impenetrable, is forced into action.

Props in the film are of great narrative importance. Of course, the Ring, both a prop and a character (or extension of one), is the most powerful in the story. We first see the Ring's power to render its wearer invisible at Bilbo's birthday party in *The Fellowship....* Here he uses it for a seemingly innocuous purpose, a dramatic exit from his own party. However, increasingly the Ring is imbued with its own personality, a whispering voice, and as the film puts it, 'a will of its own'. It is often shot in close up, which emphasises its importance despite its small physical size, the use of visuals and sound blended to give it immense power throughout the three films. Its ultimate destruction is the conclusion of the story. In the absence of a human villain it represents human desires and is therefore useful in its production of meaning beyond its physical form.

The symbolism of jewellery is also in evidence when Arwen gives her necklace to Aragorn, who wears it as a symbol of their love (and Frodo for the most part carries the Ring on a chain around his neck). But there are many other props, and as in the fantasy genre as a whole, many are imbued with magical powers, and many of them are gifts (in keeping with the Proppian analysis of stories and the use of the donor). Bilbo gives Frodo the Ring, but also other important gifts, for example, Sting, the sword. This is then used to signal the approach of danger at several points (in the Mines of Moria, at the end of *The Fellowship...* as the Urak Hai approach, and in *The Return...* as Sam rescues Frodo). He also donates his armour, and it saves Frodo's life when he is speared by a cave troll in *The Fellowship...* (it also allows for

Weaponry can accentuate character traits - the vicious hacking of the Urak Hai blade and the elegant bow of Legolas

narrative tension in that we, and the other characters, do not know he is wearing it). The last magical prop essential to Frodo and Sam is the Phial of Galadriel, a gift from Galadriel to Frodo in *The Fellowship...*, brandished by first Frodo and then Sam (along with Sting) against the giant spider Shelob in *The Return....*

SPECIAL EFFECTS

The use of complex techniques and effects to make the 'unfilmable' story of *The Lord of the Rings* films a reality is a vital element in the success and style of the films. As previously discussed, there is an argument that an emphasis on visual effects has been to the detriment of classical Hollywood narrative. *The Lord of the Rings*, with its immensely detailed world and lengthy story would not be possible or narratively credible without the extensive use of effects. Fundamental to this emphasis on spectacle for diegetic realism is the advancement of special effects, and computer-generated imagery (CGI) as well as a host of more traditional effects techniques which are central

to *The Lord of the Rings* films. From entirely computer-generated characters (Gollum, Treebeard, Sauron's eye) to enhanced props (a glowing Ring) and impossible landscapes morphed onto real locations, the use of advanced technology is ironically exactly how this other, ancient world seems believable.

'The indistinguishable nature of digital imagery and unlimited aesthetic potential of computer animation techniques have... led to a new register of illusionist spectacle'.[63] This statement may seem to offer an insight into the ways in which digital effects contribute to the cinematic experience, but why should this matter and just how new is it? Effects, of many sorts, have been central to cinema since its inception (think of George Méliès). Should they be guilty pleasures as we relish the enormity and grandeur of Middle Earth? No, it is the cinematic nature of the films that gives them much of their power. Unlike the sci-fi/action films so commonly cited to lament this emphasis on visual pleasure over narrative, the effects within *The Lord of the Rings* are so constant and range so greatly in

NOTES:

63. ibid., p164

transparency that they must be broken down into smaller sections. Perhaps the films can be regarded as an exemplary example of the combination of narrative and spectacle. Without the use of effects a fantasy film of such depth could not be fantastical at all, therefore the two would appear to form an interdependent relationship.

As with the shooting of the films, the effects did not come from Hollywood sources, but from Weta, Peter Jackson's Wellington-based effects company (once again differentiating the films from a more 'standard' Hollywood blockbuster). Watching the additional documentaries on the DVDs provides access to demystifying information about just how many different techniques were used in the films, and also about how seemingly invisible effects were so constant they become an integral part of the mise-en-scène. This element of fan partipication is now standard – part of the thrill of the effects in the cinema is in the 'how did they do that?' element, intrigue fed by DVD documentaries. An emphasis on 'new' effects is inevitably a selling point, so that while spectacle may have combined successfully with narrative within the films it must be acknowledged that the impact of ground-breaking effects is appealing to fans in its own right, enabling more intricate and complex levels of reception and participation.

This new way of approaching effects increases the films' parallels with the original *Star Wars* trilogy, whose revolutionary use of effects still stands up today. However, one of the most repeated criticisms of Lucas' most recent *Star Wars* films was the overwhelming, constant use of digital effects and blue screen work which was seen to impede the performances of the actors. With *The Lord of the Rings*, perhaps at least in part due to the organic nature of Middle Earth versus outer space, this is not the case, despite their enormous use of effects. Overt technological emphasis, say a huge amount of effects in one scene and none in another, would have jarred with the

attempt at verisimilitude. What makes the films so unique is precisely the way in which they maintain a high degree of convincing spectacle but only as narratively necessary.

Having a central dramatic character as an entirely CGI creation was unprecedented. Gollum may have been CGI, but his movements were 'motion captured' from the actor Andy Serkis, who acted within the scenes with other characters, at least partly explaining the seamlessness with which he is framed (no awkward eyeline matches here). 3D modelling was another technique used, and in fact modelling and miniatures played a large part in creating the 'realism' of the films. Gollum is unlike the majority of previous CGI creations – he is not an alien (like, for example, Jar-Jar Binks in *The Phantom Menace*) and a potentially constant problem might well have been the interruption of the diegesis through the presence of a CGI character alone, which is presumably why the details of his physicality were so vital, to move beyond this. The audience may enjoy marvelling at his sallow skin texture, his willowy hair and spindly limbs; but they must also believe in him as a fully fleshed character or the pivotol emotional storyline would not work. He, without doubt, needed to be the most integrated effect in the films to sufficiently demonstrate the disparate emotional side of his character(s).

Gollum is not the only CGI character; Treebeard also needed to be a walking talking creature (albeit with less emphasis on 'realism', as Gollum's face, skin, etc., all needed to conform on some level to human characteristics). Added to these dramatic characters are innumerable other CGI creations in the form of the fantasical beasts. Many of the 'evil' creatures of Middle Earth are computer-generated, such as the giant squid, the cave troll, the fiery balrog in the Mines of Moria (complete with audacious and impressive heat-distorted visuals), to the wargs (who attack those fleeing to Helm's Deep in

The Two Towers) complete with fur, the giant oliphaunts and Shelob, the monstrous spider. This is not mentioning the countless, literally thousands, of digital extras each able to move of their own accord (via Massive computer software, designed by Weta) during the awesome battle sequences. The list could continue. The point is that by using state of the art effects, these creatures seem 'real' and therefore their presentation does not detract from the ancient world of Middle Earth. Had they been less well done, they could very easily have jarred against the audience immersion in the diegetic world. As one of the technical crew states on *The Fellowship...* extended DVD, they wanted to erase their tracks and for audiences to say 'Effects? What effects?', such was the emphasis on the invisibility of the technical effort in order to create artificial simplicity.

Size in the films is of enormous importance. It is easy to focus on the use of CGI alongside shots of the landscape to form the vast space of Middle Earth and to overlook one fundamental use of all manner of devices: the characters in the story are of different sizes. The hobbits are meant to be approximately three feet tall but of human proportions, Gimli is a dwarf played by a strapping six foot one Welsh actor (John Rhys-Davies), yet other characters appear of 'normal' size in comparison. To an extent this is one of the reasons why the books were considered so unfilmable. The film makes use of forced perspective, an old technique that involves placing one actor further away from the camera than the other, making them seem smaller (as used in *The Fellowship...* as Frodo talks to Gandalf on the cart). *The Lord of the Rings* took this one step further by using moving forced perspective. There was also the inventive use of body doubles (Aragorn's double to work with the hobbits was over seven feet tall), large and small, as well as the replication of sets in under and over-sized versions (a good example of which is Bilbo's home, Bag End).

NOTES:

The miniature models enabled close ups of intricate architecture, so fundamental to much of the detail of the civilisations and locations and the sense of history. The elaborate towers of Isengard and Barad-dûr, for example, or the Black Gate of Mordor, involved models based on the detailed drawings of Alan Lee. The term 'miniature' is at times slightly misleading – both a thirty-fifth and a quarter-size version of Helm's Deep were built – but their integration into the story as well as digital effects are undeniably impressive.

The two main battle scenes, Helm's Deep and Pelennor Fields, can be analysed in detail for their use of different effects (as well as editing, camera, sound, music, etc.) and how these elements combine to create set-pieces (these, more than any other moments in the films, are the spectacular set-pieces brought about by narrative tension). Both use combinations of models, digital extras, digital effects and locations, stunts, even entirely computer-generated horses and an army of ghosts in the latter to amplify the level of visual impact. If effects are integrated within the narrative almost constantly, the film still successfully uses the conventions of the effects movie here by creating compulsive, occasionally horrific lengthy scenes that stand alone yet are essential to the outcome of the story.

One of the most significant 'invisible' but fundamental effects used was digital grading. This involved the conversion of 35mm film into digital format to be manipulated with computer software, and then reconverted to 35mm. The manipulation was of the lightness (or darkness) and colours of Middle Earth, for example, the adding of bluer skies, greener fields (used for Hobbiton) or the dulling of light or highlighting of a particular character's face or eyes. This dulling of light is evident in the almost monochrome scenes within the Mines of Moria, where any warmth was erased to enhance the mood. In many of the locations, from Rivendell to Lothlórien and Mordor, the scenes are evidently tinted in

particular ways, either to emphasise an ethereal quality or to darken the mood of the film. As indicated on the extended DVD this was done for 70 per cent of *The Fellowship...* and it must be assumed this level of manipulation may well have continued, yet one more way in which the familiar yet otherworldly landscape of Middle Earth could be realised by the use of technology.

To continue to list all of the effects within the films would be firstly impossible but also repetitive – much of the information regarding these is available to viewers in the multitude of extended DVD documentaries and books around the artwork of the films. What is important for the purpose of this Guide is that we appreciate the way in which the use of special effects in *The Lord of the Rings* is above and beyond many contemporary effects-driven blockbusters and therefore problematises the tendency in film theory to polarise narrative and spectacle. In these films there are in essence no pauses between effects, they are more or less continuous. The net effect of this is perhaps down to the interpretation of each viewer – either an exhausting bombardment of relentless digital incident, or the most satisfying integration yet of visual effects within a narrative entertainment.

Gandalf in Bag End, an example of on-set special effects

NOTES:

Audiences and Institutions

As related in Origins, *The Lord of the Rings* project was initially backed by Miramax Films (the company's then two executives,[64] Bob and Harvey Weinstein, are credited as Associate Producers on each of the three films). After Miramax wanted the books to be made as one film, Jackson and co. interested New Line Cinema in adapting them into three films. It is worth noting that these two companies, who devoted considerable resources to 'the biggest independent movies ever made', are by far the biggest *Hollywood* independent film companies. Their track records and survival tactics have been very similar, 'by consistently developing movies with the potential to cross over beyond the art house market'.[65]

New Line's gamble of making all three films back to back was an enormous one. Should *The Fellowship...* perform poorly, it could prove a loss of quite gigantic proportions, with the film production budgets alone totalling almost $300m. However, filming all three simultaneously would save money on crew and it was also a canny way to avoid the pitfalls of budget increases so common to sequels. With characters firmly established in audiences' minds, actors are in a strong negotiating position when signing up for a sequel and therefore salary costs, and subsequently budgets, tend to escalate dramatically. This was side-stepped by *The Lord of the Rings* by concurrent filming.

Additionally, as can happen with franchises, the star factor of the actors concerned increased to render them bigger stars with more box-office appeal for each instalment (previously unknown cast members such as Orlando Bloom have enjoyed rapid rises to fame on the back of the films). There was always the potential, therefore, that what may have seemed a very risky strategy could, and indeed did, prove astute and extremely forward-thinking, with the annual release of the films creating 'event' movies for three years running.

However, New Line and Jackson had a lot to do before the films were released or even made to ensure their word of mouth was positive, and they have continuously proved extremely shrewd. While many contemporary films go into production with little or minimal fan-knowledge (from trade press, websites, film magazines, etc.), *The Lord of the Rings* films were hotly debated and anticipated from the moment their production was announced. Peter Jackson, a relatively unknown director (albeit with a few 'cult' films to his name) took measures to ensure all-important good 'word of mouth', or rather 'word of mouse', from the beginning.

'*Lord of the Rings* fans have been actively courted by Jackson and New Line Cinema throughout all aspects of authoring, casting, filming and marketing the trilogy.'[66] In 1998 (during pre-production) Jackson offered fans the chance to ask him 20 questions about the films via the internet site www.aintitcoolnews.com. From thousands of entries he selected and answered 20, providing details about the plans in a way quite unprecedented. This tactic seemed to work to allay fears. Jackson's 'hands on' approach to film-making was being reflected in an equally hands on approach to his audience. Shying away from the extreme secrecy associated with Lucas's new *Star Wars* films, Jackson was allying himself with Tolkien fans by taking their concerns and views seriously, as well as placing himself alongside them as a fan himself. This is a microcosmic view into what at least may partly have appealed to the general public about the whole of *The Lord of the Rings* phenomenon – they did not feel patronised, force-fed or manipulated. New Line, Weta and Jackson seemed to be providing a new way of interacting with their audience as competent and discerning customers. Given the tendency for big-budget films to appeal to formulaic lowest common-denominators, this approach was unique. This also highlights the power of the internet as communal forum for communication and

debate but also as a bridge between the closed-doors nature of film production and the fansites filled with snippets of gossip and information. The producers had acknowledged this and taken control of the situation.

However, the films needed to appeal to more than just Tolkien fans, given their budget. They needed to attract large numbers of mainstream cinema-goers. Also, they had employed the risky strategy of making all films at once. Should *The Fellowship...* fail, the entire trilogy could have become one of the biggest disasters in cinema history. It is difficult in retrospect to fully grasp the risk taken as with hindsight it has become part of the mythology surrounding the films themselves.

CINEMA RELEASES

The three films employed a very simple but effective release strategy by being released annually immediately before Christmas (a holiday period, one often used to release big budget family films to maximise audiences/profit), from 2001 to 2003. This co-ordinated, annual approach was only possible because the three films had been made simultaneously – even with successful trilogies such as *Star Wars* the sequel needed to be made after the release of the first film, rendering such a tight release date impossible. The feverish anticipation of the first film in 2001 was equalled only by the anticipation for another adaptation of a phenomenally successful franchise of fantasy children's books, Harry Potter. *The Fellowship...* and *Harry Potter and the Philosopher's* (or *Scorcerer's* in the US) *Stone* (2001) were being discussed in the trade, broadsheet and tabloid press as rivals. Held to be of similar genres (the Harry Potter saga being influenced by Tolkien) and believed to have similar audiences, how would the two compare in their ability to attract audiences? While the Harry Potter film could be argued to be more child-centric, the books have had enormous cross-over appeal with adults. *The*

NOTES:

64. The Weinsteins left Miramax, now a wholly owned subsidiary of Disney, in the autumn of 2005.

65. Neale, *Contemporary Hollywood Cinema*, 1998, p76

66. Shefrin, E, 'Lord of the Rings, Star Wars and Mapping Participatory Fandom', *Critical Studies in Media Communication*, Vol 21 No 3

Lord of the Rings books are appreciated as both adult and children's books, with the films being notably more violent yet still passable as 'family films'. This competition is useful in comparing release strategies, but is also worth noting for other pertinent reasons.

The Fellowship... was very much perceived as the more 'independent' film, with **Harry Potter...** being seen as the more commercial studio release. **Harry Potter...** was indeed made by Warner Brothers, a major Hollywood studio, **The Lord of the Rings** by New Line Cinema (a 'major independent'). Yet *both* are owned by the over-arching conglomerate, TimeWarner. So, in effect, they were at least on some levels produced by the same organisation. This seems entirely at odds with the way in which they were presented as rivals. This is not to suggest that there was a cynical obscuring of this fact, rather it highlights the vertically and horizontally integrated nature of today's media conglomerates and the invisibility of ownership to consumers. This could be argued to be media imperialism, with what appears to be choice and market competition being, in fact, merely different branding – different routes to the same ends (shareholder profits).

In other respects, however, **The Lord of the Rings** maintains the status of independent production. New Line Cinema was independent enough that it did not use the studio's global distribution network. The distribution rights to **The Lord of the Rings** films were negotiated by territory to domestic distributors. In the UK the distributor was Entertainment. This is a British-owned distribution house (i.e. not a multinational studio or conglomerate), one with a string of successful films under its belt such as the Austin Powers franchise (also produced by New Line). It is a bit of an anomaly, and therefore very interesting, in that it successfully distributes relatively large films domestically. A similar pattern was repeated elsewhere, with Metropolitan distributing the

films in France and FilmAuro in Italy, with Warner Brothers acting as distributor in other major territories (Germany, for example) and New Line's domestic distribution arm handling the films in the US.

The Fellowship... was released in 16 international territories on 16 December 2001, five more on December 20 and Australia on 26 December.[67] This was a month after the release of **Harry Potter...**, giving both films the window to open without counter-productively splitting audiences. **The Fellowship...** took over $60m in its first five days of release and went on to take $350m worldwide in its first two weeks[68], thus recouping the trilogy's entire production budget in that time (but not the expensive hidden costs such as potentially $50m for marketing per film). The trade press and film magazines are often filled with fanfares of huge openings. What such figures often fail to account for is either the costs of the size of the release – more prints equals more screenings and therefore more money but also more expense to have the prints made. It also fails to take into account what can happen afterwards – a very rapid drop-off of box-office if the film fails to gain positive word of mouth. A big release may therefore be the way in which some films make back most of their costs, but even having been trumpeted as having 'one of the biggest openings ever', may drop off and ultimately perform less well than expected (**The Matrix Reloaded** (2003) is a prime example of this). When a film has 'legs', it will continue to have box-office appeal for an extended period. Usually a film's takings will decline over time, sometimes dramatically, sometimes more slowly. But no matter how much hype and publicity are pumped into a release, some films capture the public imagination and some do not.

Where this relates to **The Fellowship...** is that its box-office figures actually *rose* after its opening weekend. In the UK (a well-known prime market for fantasy films, for example

As the focus of the films' narrative shifted, so did the poster art. Frodo was at the centre of all the promotion for **The Fellowship...** but by the time of **The Return...** he was one character amongst many, with Aragorn dominating

NOTES:

67. Screen International, 1 January 2002, p43
68. ibid.

the original **Star Wars** films here out-performed most other countries) they rose by 7 per cent[69] on its second weekend. This was a pattern repeated across countries such as Germany and (of course) New Zealand, Australia and even territories such as South Korea showed enormous box-office admissions.

Ultimately the film took less than the first **Harry Potter...** internationally (**Harry Potter** took $966,700,000 worldwide, **The Fellowship...** took $859,900,000).[70] The subsequent **Lord of the Rings** films, however, remedied this. It may have won on box-office, but critically, **Harry Potter...** was not as well received, and much of its appeal was seen to be for children rather than adults. Jackson's status as cult auteur seemed to be paying off, and his film was seen as far darker than Chris Columbus's take on J.K. Rowling's book. **The Fellowship...** won four Golden Globe and thirteen Oscar nominations, winning four of the latter. Also important to note, and this is applicable to all three **Lord of the Rings** films, is that by being released in December their annual box-office take would be divided over two years, therefore splitting their total on paper and not necessarily accurately reflecting the overall take of any one of the films over a particular year.

The surge of popularity of both **Harry Potter...** and **The Fellowship...** gave the cinema industry a much-needed boost (the films were released very soon after 9/11 at a time when many, more conventional Hollywood action films were considered problematic in their sudden resemblance to current events) and also acted as franchise launches. It is difficult now to look back and see **The Fellowship...** as the underdog but in essence it was, not being perceived as a studio release and with less contemporary currency than the Harry Potter saga. Harry Potter's fourth book instalment cannily came out at a similar time to the first film, emphasising cross-media convergence (considered in more detail later).

The subsequent releases inevitably benefited enormously from the success of the first film and by the fact that from that moment on they were going to be hotly anticipated, and this time a known quantity in the public consciousness, giving them a ready-made audience in a similar way to sequels. The star profile of the actors involved was rising with each instalment (and in the case of particular actors due to the concurrent release of other franchises, for example Hugo Weaving in **The Matrix**, Ian McKellen in the **X-Men** franchise and Orlando Bloom in **Pirates of the Caribbean** (2003)). The timing of the releases utilised the marketing of the 'event' movies, and the successive two became arguably the most anticipated films of their year, further aided by the release of the extended DVD versions shortly before each new instalment.

The Two Towers, released on 18 December 2002 took more than both **The Fellowship...** and **Harry Potter and the Chamber of Secrets** (released again a month prior), taking $926,287,400 (close to an American $ billion) worldwide to **Chamber**'s $876,688,482. Its five-day opening was 38 per cent higher than **The Fellowship**'s, taking $87.9m. By **The Return...**, released 17 December 2003, the competition was in effect over, with the third Harry Potter film not released until the following summer. The third part of an ongoing franchise could not and would not compete with the final instalment of what was by this point one of cinema's most financially successful undertakings. **The Return...** outperformed them all, taking a phenomenal $1,118,887,224 67. This meant that the three films, with a production budget of $300m, a marketing campaign of probably half of that amount again (as well as release costs etc.), grossed almost $3 billion in their cinema releases alone. Added to this the DVD sales, product tie-ins and merchandising, it becomes clear that what New Line, Weta, *et al.*, achieved is simply staggering. And despite the lack of a cinema release in 2004 there was the Special Extended Version on DVD, released

on 10 December, to at least partially perpetuate the saga – and the income stream.

Not only does such a box-office figure indicate that huge numbers of people flocked to see the films, but as with **Titanic**, some went again and again, and would then buy the DVD, and watch that again and again. The magnitude of the success of the films is astounding, and in keeping with movie myth, what was one of cinema's biggest gambles really did hit the jackpot in a way perhaps even those behind it may not have foreseen.

The final instalment also finally garnered the critical acknowledgement of the establishment, winning each of the 11 Academy Awards for which it was nominated, generally perceived as an acknowledgement of the artistic and commercial success of the entire project.

THE DVD RELEASES

Not content with establishing a new pattern for theatrical releases, **The Lord of the Rings** reinforced it when it came to the other (and increasingly more profitable) main arena for film consumption, the DVD. Standard DVD releases tend to occur approximately six months after the cinematic release (six months was previously considered the appropriate 'window' to allow exhibitors potentially long runs but which has been eroded in recent years). The DVD in itself is an entirely different dimension to the experience of film. On the one hand the vast spectacle of cinema is lost, as is the communal experience of cinema-going. But on the other, the viewer of a DVD is in far more control, and increasingly DVDs have meant the incorporation of additional features as standard.

Uniquely at that time, each of the three **Lord of the Rings** films enjoyed two DVD releases, each several months apart. One was the theatrical version, the other a longer 'director's cut', again something previously unheard of in such a carefully structured way.

NOTES:

69. Screen International, 4 Jan, 2002
70. www.boxofficemojo.com

Related to the positioning of Jackson as new Hollywood auteur is the specific stamp he has put on the subsequent DVD releases: 'Is the director's cut a return to the original vision of the auteur-director, freed from whatever compromises were involved in the initial release? Or just a cynical marketing ploy? It could be both…What the phenomenon of the director's cut version implies, however, is the role of a commodified version of auteurism continues to play in Hollywood's industrial calculations and marketing strategies.'[71] Each Special Extended Edition comes in a suitably organic, ancient-looking faux-leather box, green for *The Fellowship...*, brown for *The Two Towers*, and dark (royal?) blue for *The Return....* Internal graphics use conceptual drawings from the films, all emphasising authenticity, despite the medium's reliance on modern technology, similar to the actual text's presentation of Middle Earth.

Once more the unique production, distribution and exhibition pattern is worth analysing. The Special Extended Editions not only offer a barrage of 'making ofs' to feed the fans interested in deconstructing the creative processes behind the films, but far more importantly they offer new versions of the films themselves. They have been presented as the films that would have been shown theatrically had industrial conventions regarding length of cinema releases not had to apply (*The Fellowship...* in its extended version is 30 minutes longer, *The Two Towers* 43 minutes longer, both just under three hours in their cinematic releases; the final instalment ran over three hours in the cinema and over *four* in the extended version). This is interesting for several reasons. Firstly, because it openly acknowledges, and utilises, the different viewing experiences offered by DVD to the cinema (the method of watching is entirely at the discretion of the individual in his or her private sphere). Secondly, it elevates this cult of the DVD collector and provides it with a product designed specifically for that audience (there is now a *five* disc as well as

four disc edition available of the films). This niche market was being catered for on a large scale. Different versions of the same film were being created that openly acknowledged not only differing viewing patterns but different audience wants and needs. While some viewers may have found the cinematic releases quite long enough and seen them in a similar way to other blockbusters, others would have felt the desire to always 'see more', a factor which accounts for a large amount of the appeal of DVD in the first place. The promise of additional minutes (an enormous 50 extra minutes for the third film) also meant that following the cinema release there was actually still a further, more 'complete' version to see, once more maintaining audience interest. By making clear these intentions from the outset New Line were also able to capitalise on the perspective of these additional elements being for 'fans', rather than as cynical add-ons.

So not only were numerous extras added, but previously unseen footage was integrated into the films, with new musical scores, effects and so forth created especially which allows the releases to seem once again more like films made *by* fans *for* fans than for purely commercial gain. The idea of directors' cuts have had varied success, and the majority if not all have been created in retrospect rather than concurrently. So how did these films manage to walk the tightrope between mainstream commercialism (tie-ins with Burger King, huge amounts of merchandising, computer games, etc.) and maintain some form of 'integrity' essential for appealing to a more discerning audience?

With the case of the extended release the implication was that they were not just an afterthought but considered a highly legitimate product in their own right. They were offering added value. Cynically, of course, it is fundamentally an additional release of the film (each film therefore having three releases within a 12 month cycle – cinema version, 2-disc cinema version DVD,

and 4-disc extended DVD). On the other hand each extended release would have come at some considerable production costs. This would be off-set by the generation not only of additional revenue but interest and word of mouth for the subsequent instalment's theatrical release. It was an excellent marketing strategy:

TIMELINE OF CINEMA AND DVD RELEASES FOR *THE LORD OF THE RINGS*

The Fellowship of the Ring
Theatrical release 16 December 2001
DVD release (theatrical, 2 discs) 6 August 2002
DVD release (extended, 4 discs) 12 November 2002

The Two Towers
Theatrical release 18 December 2002
DVD release (theatrical, 2 discs) 26 August 2003
DVD release (extended, 4 discs) 18 November 2003

The Return of the King
Theatrical release 17 December 2003
DVD release (theatrical, 2 discs) 25 May 2004
DVD release (extended, 4 discs) 10 December 2004

Christmas theatrical releases of the films therefore benefited from the November DVD release of the extended previous instalment; without the theatrical version on DVD released over the summer the public's interest may well have waned, and so this trio of releases reinforced the films in the public consciousness and symbiotically increased the appeal of each subsequent instalment. So they forged and maximised a mutual marketing and publicity strategy planned with such precision and executed on an annual basis that the public was not only expecting each release, they were anticipating it and the one that followed. As previously stated this could only have been done

NOTES:

71. www.boxofficemojo.com

with all three films being made concurrently, and therefore the unique pattern of production gave rise to this unique pattern of distribution and consumption.

The significantly earlier release of **The Return...** on DVD, at the end of May 2004, can be seen as relating to the enormous success of the film at the Academy Awards in February. Also, with no new instalment to be released theatrically, the Special Extended Edition DVD release was pushed back to December, presumably to capitalise on the gap in the event movie schedule left by the cycle having concluded (as well as, of course, offering a rather appealing Christmas gift for the devotee).

Merchandising

With the cinema and DVD releases New Line/Jackson seem to have achieved the impossible in simultaneously appeasing Tolkien fans, attracting hoards of new audiences and also managing to act as commercial blockbuster with all the product tie-ins and affiliations that routinely accompany such releases. Running a promotional partnership with Burger King would, one may think, detract from the quality of the films in the eyes of come cinema-goers. Yet this did not happen. While it is easy to say that it is the power of the film-making that has rendered this seemingly impossible feat feasible, the patterns of consumption associated with it must also be discussed. One issue it may highlight is the audience awareness and, importantly, the acceptance of conventions associated with large-budget releases as cultural products.

The Lord of the Rings films saturated the market with tie-ins. All these followed the key art that had been created for the films, and there were numerous teaser and quad posters, featuring a range of characters, but all with muted organic colours in keeping with the 'ancient' world of Middle Earth (and the 'main' posters feature the key characters and

act as ensemble posters in a similar way to the original key art for **Star Wars**). Merchandising such as the **Star Wars**-esque figurines to mugs, mouse mats, posters, playing cards, collectable cards, clothing, books, board games, masks, stamps, even pipes and rings are just a few that carried the endorsement (and visual style) of the films. Not to mention the creation by EA Games of the affiliated computer games on all formats (X Box, PC, Game Cube, Playstation 2, etc.) for each instalment. The highly lucrative world of gaming now at times exceeds the box-office take of the source 'text' and while it did not in this instance it would have nonetheless added considerably to the total income for the franchise. The nature of the gaming experience is one that increasingly impacts on films as texts themselves, with the 'player' able to control their own narrative in an immersive environment rather than passively observe the experiences of others. Where Jackson's lone auteur image and cottage industry methodology become problematic is where this convergence of media forms and such merchandising is concerned. To create such an all-encompassing cross-media experience in an era of globalisation you need access to cross-media ownership. The conglomerate TimeWarner has access to an enormous range of cross-media outlets, therefore it must be acknowledged that while the films may not have abided by standard Hollywood rules of vertical integration, some amount of horizontal integration is evident in their merchandising and promotion.

Lastly and by no means least is the knock-on effect of Jackson's films and their impact on his home country. Despite much of this book looking at the creation of Middle Earth as a mythical place, tourism in New Zealand has rocketed since the release of the films. One could argue that the aerial shots and breath-taking views so often used by the films are in themselves an advert for the nearest thing we have to Middle Earth, and as such tourists may now visit the 'real' places featured in the

films, offering an immersive 'experience'. New Zealand's involvement in the production process is also inevitably a way in which the films have been seen as being apart from Hollywood (in a positive way), using local crews, technical experts, actors, extras and, of course, locations. Wellington was even re-named Middle Earth for the premiere of the first film, and Jackson was there in person to address the crowds (does the man ever sleep?).

The films do seem to have managed to successfully appeal as different experiences for diverse audiences. The perceived 'high' cultural value of the books (in some quarters, although never quite as elevated in the literary canon as amongst 'ordinary' audiences) appears to have been maintained more or less intact for those who wished it preserved; yet the films have worked as contemporary blockbusters with all the mass-consumption that implies. The films as a phenomenon therefore bring to the fore the very notions of cultural value and 'taste', and the postmodern collapsing of these categories fascinatingly embodied by **The Lord of the Rings**.

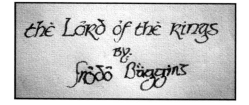

NOTES:

72. King, *New Hollywood Cinema*, 2002

NARRATIVE

The term **narrative** describes not only the story element of films, but also *how* the story is presented to us.

- What, in your opinion, is *The Lord of the Rings* about?

This may seem obvious but one of the primary purposes of stories in cultures has been recognised to be how we make sense of the world by reducing complexities to more simple ideas. So stories, even simple ones, have meaning. Often good and evil, for example, are the two extremes around which a story is based. They also can all have similar patterns. This is a good starting point for looking at narrative.

Narrative can be broken down into three main elements – **time**, **space** and **causality**. Time is when the story takes place; space is where; and causality is why. Whilst this may seem easy, again it is how these elements are established that makes narrative interesting to study.

TASK – Looking at time, space and cause

Each of the films uses a Prologue – a section at the opening of the film before the story actually begins. The first of these is an excellent starting point for looking at these three basic narrative elements.

- Watch the prologue to *The Fellowship of the Ring*.

Now think about how the three main elements of narrative are constructed – TIME, SPACE and CAUSE. How are these established in the sequence? Make notes on each in the table below. You can watch the sequence more than once.

Time	Space	Cause

EXTENSION TASK – Narration and Depth of Knowledge

Narration uses different techniques for different ends. For instance in a thriller, often the audience will know only as much as the characters on screen to create surprise as events unfold. This is called **restricted** narration (literally, when the audience has their knowledge restricted). Another technique is **unrestricted**, or **omniscient** narration, when suspense can be created by what the audience knows in comparison to the characters on screen.

A good example of a film that uses **restricted** knowledge is *The Matrix* (1999), where the audience is kept in the dark with Neo about what 'the matrix' is until dramatic information is suddenly revealed; or a film like *Scream* (1996) where the killer's identity is not revealed until near the end of the film – and importantly in both cases we find out at the same time as the main character in the film does.

Unrestricted/omniscient knowledge is used in combination with restricted in most cases. So for example at the opening of *American Beauty* (1999) we are told by the title character that he will be dead in less than a year, and we have previously witnessed a girl (his daughter) discussing killing him, meaning we have unrestricted knowledge because the characters, as soon as the action starts, do not know this themselves. Yet we do not know why or how he dies, and this is restricted narration.

It is most common for films to use a combination of both methods, to create both surprise (if for example we see a character drink something and then die, we are surprised and assume they were poisoned) and suspense (if we know the drink is poisoned and witness a character about to drink it, we are in suspense).

TASK

- Thinking about *The Lord of the Rings*, can you decide which device is used in the films? Or is it a combination? Try and consider why the techniques were used.

- Look at the Prologue to the first film once more, as well as the following sequence in Hobbiton. In terms of knowledge about events, how does this affect the audience vs. character knowledge? What effect does it have on the audience that we know of the Ring when none of the characters do?

- If you now watch the openings of the other two films you will see each also has a Prologue that takes places before the action of the story actually starts. Consider the function of the Prologues. Are they the same, and if not how do they differ and why in you opinion?

NARRATIVE

The Three–Act Structure

A narrative theorist, Tzvetan Todorov, analysed the construction of narrative as a three-act structure. He believed there was in each narrative:

equilibrium – disequilibrium – new equilibrium

Equilibrium would be often where 'safety' is established, as well as the principal characters. Events occur which bring about **disequilibrium**, or a state where something has happened to set off the beginning of the story action. In order to reach the final **new equilibrium**, obstacles must be overcome.

TASK

- What is the **equilibrium** in **The Lord of the Rings** taken as one continuous narrative? How long does it last? It is often considered that the equilibrium at the opening of a film must be a *false* equilibrium (if everything were truly in equilibrium nothing would have to happen at all, dramatically speaking). Is a false equilibrium evident?

- How is **disequilibrium** brought about? How long does it last?

- Finally, what is the **new equilibrium** and how is it achieved?

  (TIP: If you consider the narrative of all three films as one, it can often help to plot a list of events to see how the story moves forward.)

EXTENSION TASK

Having thought about **The Lord of the Rings** films as one narrative we can now look at them individually – they are of course a trio of films. Film viewers will still have certain expectations for each individual film, which must in a sense stand on its own right as an independent film.

EXTENSION TASK

- How do you think the film-makers have made each film follow the three act rule? Bear in mind you do not need to be absolutely specific – it is an exercise to demonstrate whether such narrative rules can be applied to the films individually.

As the films progress inevitably they move away from the structure of equilibrium-disequilibrium-new equilibrium. For example, at the conclusion of **The Two Towers**, Gollum leads an unknowing Frodo and Sam towards some dark fate. We, the audience, know this whereas the characters do not (unrestricted/omniscient narration), however our knowledge is still also restricted (we don't know what Gollum talks about, only what his plan is) so the film ends on a disequilibrium. So, does the film manage to abide by a three-act structure? And how will it being the second of three films affect audience expectation?

NARRATIVE

Characters, Functions and Narrative

Narrative can be broken down into elements. **Cause**, the reasons for stories and events moving forward, is most often created by **characters** within the stories (villains for example). Characters often have traits that are of particular relevance to the story. Russian folklorist Vladimir Propp said of folktales that despite the number or seeming difference of these stories, there are a finite number of character functions that are easily categorisable from story to story. This idea, of **character function**, can be another useful way of analysing narratives. It can help to explain why audiences will have expectations before they have even seen a film – they will expect a certain pattern, certain character types and so on.

DISCUSSION TASK

- Think about what you **expect** when you go to see a film. Do you always expect to see a story?

TASK – Character functions

Below are listed the seven main character functions that Propp identified. Let's find out if it works by trying to apply these to *The Lord of the Rings*.

- Who, in your opinion, performs the character functions listed? Bear in mind there can be more than one character for each function, and similarly one character can have more than one function.

The villain	
The donor (gives something to hero)	
The helper (aids hero)	
The princess (and her father)	
The dispatcher (sends hero away)	
The hero	
The false hero	

EXTENSION TASK

- Consider other films you have seen in relation to these character functions. A good example is *Star Wars* (1977).

GENRE

Genre tends to mean a group or type of films with similarities e.g. we can recognise a romantic comedy or science fiction film by certain formal qualities.

For example, in the case of science fiction films:

Setting   Often futuristic / Space, other planets etc, spaceships

Characters   Scientists, robots and so on

Costume   Again often futuristic, unfamiliar, showy, foregrounding design

Weaponry   Laser guns etc

Transport   Spacecraft. All of the above may foreground/special effects

If you look at, the Western, you would come up with an entirely different set of generic patterns – the Wild West, cowboys, horses as transport, etc. These are the **iconographic** ways of looking at genre.

But genre has a further function, which is to create audience familiarity. If you think about it, each time we pay money to see a film we are paying for something we don't know if we will like or enjoy. It's like buying an item of clothing without trying it on. So genre is used by the industry to make us feel more like we know what we are paying for.

TASK

- List some of the last films you've seen.

- Try and categorise them in terms of genre – horror, Westerns and so on.

- Now think about HOW you came to these decisions (conventions, similarity to other films, the film poster, etc.).

The point with genre is that it is far easier to assign a film to a category than it is to actually describe the genre itself. For example it is easier to say a film like **The Searchers** (1956) is a Western because it contains cowboys, Indians, horses and so on, than it is to describe *how* and *why* these notions of the Western as a genre have evolved, or what a Western actually is.

Further, genre is often a changing idea in itself. Nowadays many films can fit multiple genres. For example **The Matrix** (1999) is not just science fiction – it is also an action film, with elements of martial arts, influences of the comic book, and so on.

EXTENSION TASK

- Can you define **The Lord of the Rings** as a particular genre? Does it have more than one?

- Think about how you came to your conclusions – was it the content, the look of the films or how they were marketed for example?

- If you find the films difficult to categories generically, how instead do you think audiences would have understood them (think in particular about **The Fellowship of the Ring**)?

GENRE

Genre and the Blockbuster

TASK

- List any words you associate with the term blockbuster.

- Now list any films you class as blockbusters. Consider why you would call them that.

- Think about these words and films in relation to genre – are there any patterns?

- It is often argued that blockbusters are defined more by institutional factors like budgets, star presence, studio releases, merchandising and hype than actual content, and that it is a term used more often in retrospect (ie only after a film has been released can we tell if it will make a lot of money). Think about this in relation to all of the above. Do you think it's a fair assumption?

- Now think about **The Lord of the Rings** films – are they blockbusters in your opinion? Discuss this point in groups, half arguing for and half arguing against.

GENRE

The Trilogy

Generically, the phenomenon of the trilogy exists as a way of structuring films for audiences. Films like the **Scream** series, despite in effect being sequels, relied heavily on the concept of the trilogy for the marketing of **Scream 3** (1999). Similarly, some films that use the common knowledge and acceptance of the trilogy then break those rules, for example the **Alien** series, now a 'quadrilogy'.

DISCUSSION TASK

- Why, in your opinion, is the trilogy so well known and understood by audiences as a story-telling structure?

TASK

- A lot of trilogies abide by the rules of the blockbuster. Using the table below, plot the principal features of some successful trilogies:

	Star Wars (either trilogy)	*The Matrix* trilogy	*The Terminator* films	*The Lord of the Rings*
Narrative (per film and as a 'whole')				
Genre				
Characters/ Stars				
Release dates				
Audience				
Marketing/ Tagline				

GENRE

The Trilogy

EXTENSION TASKS

- Did all the films in each trilogy 'work' as elements of a trio?

- Do you think **The Lord of the Rings** films actually are a trilogy, considering the films were shot simultaneously and are in effect from one book? If they aren't, why do you think people still consider them as one? Think again in terms of genre and audience familiarity.

- While it looks as if trilogies are the domain of Hollywood, there do exist more independent trilogies, for example Krzysztof Kieslowski's **Three Colours** (1993–94) trilogy. Investigate this non-Hollywood trilogy and look at how it may differ in terms of content and meaning.

AUTEUR

Film directors are often discussed, particularly in film magazines such as Empire, as the ultimate author of a film. This attitude stems originally from the 1960s when a group of French film critics attempted to reclaim film as an artistic (rather than commercial) medium by studying the director as artist, or author (auteur means 'author' in French).

These writers were primarily looking at European directors, and in fact many of these critics became directors themselves (Truffaut, Godard and so on), as well as particular Hollywood directors (Alfred Hitchcock and Howard Hawks, for example). In the late 70s and early 80s, a group of young, ambitious Hollywood directors emerged and were identified as what is sometimes called the 'new Hollywood' auteurs – Steven Spielberg, George Lucas, Francis Ford Coppola and Martin Scorsese amongst others. This tradition, of highlighting the role of the director, is another way of creating familiarity for an audience, and more and more relates to industry and audience categorisation than necessarily genuine production processes.

TASK

- Name as many film directors/auteurs as you can.

- Now look at your list – how many are men, and how many are women?

- Discuss your findings.

- Now, why do you think the role of the film director is so important? Do you agree with auteur theory?

- Why should it follow that a director, rather than a screenwriter, or a cinematographer, should be considered an auteur?

These questions highlight the problematic nature of auteur theory. Many people are involved in the creation of films, why should a director be so much more known and praised than anyone else?

AUTEUR

If you still aren't convinced, think about this:

The job that is most often there from the beginning of a film's development, who is responsible for getting finance, talent and even appointing the director, is a producer.

- Can you name any famous producers?

Producers are often by far the most powerful people in the industry, yet often audiences do not even know what they do or who they are. This certainly gives an indication of how the idea of director as auteur is more about how audiences organise their viewing than industrial practice.

- Similarly, name some famous screenwriters. Why should they not be considered auteurs?

TASK

- In terms of **The Lord of the Rings** films, do you consider director Peter Jackson to be an auteur? List your reasons.

He was also co-producer, co-screenwriter and so on, so he did indeed have a lot of influence over many elements of the production process. However, so did his partner, Fran Walsh (she is listed as Co-Producer and Screenwriter along with Philippa Boyens).

- Would you therefore also consider Fran Walsh an auteur of the films?

- What about JRR Tolkien, the actual author of the book? Could he be argued to be the auteur?

These questions are supposed to help you question your assumptions about the status of a director, and the role of auteur theory. Like so many elements of film – genre, stardom and so on – it has become so commonplace that often it is easy to forget that these ideas are constructed.

FILM LANGUAGE

There are many sequences in the three films that are particularly useful for looking at the way film is constructed. Broadly, **mise-en-scène** (all that is placed on the screen) can be broken down into the following elements:

- Locations/Setting

- Costume

- Props

- Special Effects

- Use of Camera and Editing

- Sound and Soundtrack

How all these elements work together not only affects narrative and genre but the very important look of a film.

Thinking back to Narrative, the opening Prologue was useful in terms of how it presented information. This sequence can again be extremely useful when looking at how **The Lord of the Rings** films look.

Even though the films are set in a mythical world of Middle Earth, looking at the films and viewing the multitude of extras on the DVDs it is clear that a lot of time was spent on creating a level of realism. **Realism** is created when all elements work together to create a credible, believable world. Classical Hollywood narrative tends to use all elements to best encourage the viewer to suspend disbelief.

Location/Setting

Firstly, think about the use of **location** and **setting** in the films. Not only do these have narrative relevance (the film's story is intimately bound to locations with two extremes – The Shire and Mordor – at opposing ends for example, or locations with heights creating much tension for characters in peril), much of the look of the films relates to these locations.

TASK

- Pick a scene that introduces us to a location (e.g. the Shire, Rivendell, Gondor and so on). How is that particular location presented?

  Think about
  - Landscape
  - Use of camera (extreme long shots? Mid shots?)
  - Effects (are they visible or do they blend in?)
  - Architecture
  - Music

And so on. Do this with only a few locations/settings and you will soon see that the way they are presented is affected by these elements. You will start to see not only what is presented, but why.

Costume and Props

TASK

Choose a few characters to analyse in terms of **costume** and **props** (e.g. weaponry) and how it affects the portrayal of each in terms of how we perceive them (their 'traits'). A good example would be to look at the **Fellowship** in the first film, as they depart form Rivendell in the middle of the film:

Character	Description of Costume	Weaponry	Character's Traits?
Frodo			
Gandalf			
Aragorn/Strider			
Legolas			
Gimli			
Sam			
Pippin			
Merry			
Boromir			

You can quickly see that through the visual codes of these elements we, the viewer, gather much information without necessarily being aware of it. Iconography such as costume and props taps into our pre-existing cultural codes. A further example of this would be to compare the male character's costumes with those of the female characters. They show the constructed differences between our understandings of masculinity and femininity, and are particularly in evidence in these three films.

FILM LANGUAGE

Special Effects

There is much written about the increased prominence of special effects in commercial cinema. Particular genres lend themselves to highlighting the progress of new technology through the use of special effects.

DISCUSSION TASK

- How much do you think *The Lord of the Rings* films rely on special effects for their effectiveness?

There are several large sequences that clearly use CGI effects, however one of the interesting factors of the films is that digital manipulation is used so much it is difficult to see what is real and what is an effect. This has an impact on **realism**.

TASK

Take a look at the sequences mentioned below and see to what extent you think they contain special effects and what the effect is:

- The Battle of Helm's Deep (at the end of *The Two Towers*);

- The Battle of Pelennor Fields (the large battle sequence in *The Return of the King*).

One argument made about effects is that increasingly they are simply there for the viewer to marvel at, not to aid the narrative.

- Looking at these two sequences, do you agree?

There is one particular less 'grand' use of special effects in the films – the character of Gollum.

- Do you think he is there for the audience to 'marvel' at or does he work as a character in his own right? Think about any other entirely CGI characters on film and how they may be similar to or differ from Gollum.

FILM LANGUAGE

Use of Camera and Editing

How and what the **camera** shows us has a direct relation to how we perceive events. For example, close ups or extreme close ups on someone's face tend to signify or highlight emotion, long shots work to place characters within their surroundings.

TASK

- Textual analysis 1: The battle of Helm's Deep (***The Two Towers***)

Camera Shot	Length	Lighting/ background	Sound	Overall effect

Using the grid above as a guide, chart the sequence of shots in a short sequence from the Helm's Deep battle (this sequence in particular has been chosen because of the number and variety of camera shots). Consider how lighting and sound adds to the overall effect of the image, and record your impression of the sequence for each shot.

Use of Camera and Editing

- Textual analysis 2: The internal battle of Gollum (*The Two Towers*)

This sequence shows a clever use of camera to create an entirely different effect from a battle scene. As Sam and Frodo lie sleeping Gollum/Sméagol do battle for his will. The way it is shot makes it appear that they are two different people arguing with each other. Deconstruct the sequence to consider the following:

Camera Shot	Length	Lighting/ background	Sound	Overall effect

FILM LANGUAGE

Sound and Soundtrack

Sound on film breaks into two main categories:

- **Diegetic** sound is sound that the characters within the story world would hear (dialogue, swords clashing and so on).

- **Non-diegetic** sound it sound that only the audience can hear (e.g. the soundtrack, or a voice over). A combination of both is most often used in a film with high production values, and often a large emphasis is placed on the musical score of large budget films.

TASKS

- Think about the musical score to **The Lord of the Rings**. Is it what you would consider 'epic'? Why are film soundtracks so important, do you think?

- Now think about how the use of **diegetic** sound can add realism to films. For example if it accompanies CGI effects it makes them seem credible and three-dimensional. Look at the sequence as Saruman's army march in **The Two Towers** and how artificial extras/effects are given realism by sound.

- A good example of the use of non-diegetic sound is in the Prologue to **The Return of the King**, as we see how Sméagol became Gollum. Watch the sequence and consider how music and sound effects affect the way we witness events. Consider the moments where lack of sound is used – as Frodo is stabbed in the mines in **The Fellowship...,** or as Gandalf later falls. What impact does this technique have? Bear in mind too that the use of silence in film is important, and consider why.

AUDIENCES AND INSTITUTIONS

Production

The three films of **The Lord of the Rings** were made back to back at the same time. This meant the approval of a huge budget of $300 million, a previously unheard of amount of money to be committed to a film project (albeit three releases). This was a big gamble.

DISCUSSION TASK

- Why do you think New Line approved all three films to be made at once?

TASK

Look on www.imdb.com (the Internet Movie Database) and investigate budgets of other films you can think of (you can choose blockbusters as a good comparison if you wish). How do their budgets compare?

*N.B.: the 'hidden' under-the-line P&A costs (Prints and Advertising) of a film like **The Lord of the Rings** will be approximately $50 million per film.*

TASK

Look at the box office totals for each film below:

The Fellowship of the Ring	$871, 368, 364
The Two Towers	$926, 287, 400
The Return of the King	$1, 118, 888, 879

Why do you think the subsequent films made more than the first film? Compare the box office of these with some other trilogies (www.imdb.com under Box Office)

AUDIENCES AND INSTITUTIONS

Box Office Analysis

Each table below shows the top ten films worldwide for each year a **Lord of the Rings** instalment was released.

2001

Rank	Title	Studio	Box Office
1	*Harry Potter and the Philosopher's Stone*	Warner Bros	$976.5m
2	*The Lord of the Rings: The Fellowship of the Ring*	New Line	$870. 0m
3	*Monsters Inc.*	Buena Vista	$525.4m
4	*Shrek*	Dreamworks	$484.4m
5	*Ocean's Eleven*	Warner Bros	$450.7m
6	*Pearl Harbour*	Buena Vista	$449.2m
7	*The Mummy Returns*	Universal	$433.0m
8	*Jurassic Park III*	Universal	$368.8m
9	*Planet of the Apes*	20th Century Fox	$362.2m
10	*Hannibal*	MGM	$351.7m

2002

Rank	Title	Studio	Box Office
1	*The Lord of the Rings: The Two Towers*	New Line	$924.3m
2	*Harry Potter and the Chamber of Secrets*	Warner Bros	$876.7m
3	*Spider-Man*	Sony	$821.7m
4	*Star Wars Episode II: Attack of the Clones*	20th Century Fox	$640.9m
5	*Men in Black II*	Sony	$441.8m
6	*Die Another Day*	MGM	$432.0m
7	*Signs*	Buena Vista	$408.2m
8	*Ice Age*	20th Century Fox	$382.7m
9	*My Big Fat Greek Wedding*	IFC	$368.7m
10	*Minority Report*	20th Century Fox	$358.4m

2003

Rank	Title	Studio	Box Office
1	*The Lord of the Rings: The Return of the King*	New Line	$1,118.9m
2	*Finding Nemo*	Buena Vista	$864.5m
3	*The Matrix Reloaded*	Warner Bros	$738.6m
4	*Pirates of the Caribbean: The Curse of the Black Pearl*	Buena Vista	$653.9m
5	*Bruce Almighty*	Universal	$484.6m
6	*The Last Samurai*	Warner Bros	$456.8m
7	*Terminator 3: Rise of the Machines*	Warner Bros	$433.4m
8	*The Matrix Revolutions*	Warner Bros	$425.0m
9	*X-Men 2*	20th Century Fox	$406.4m
10	Bad Boys 2	Sony (Columbia)	$273.3m

Source: www.boxofficemojo.com

These tables can provide a lot of information and points for discussion.

TASK

- Choose one year to focus on and think about the types of genre represented in the top ten films. Are they all easy to categorise?

- If not, what other elements may have been used to create 'familiarity'? Think in particular about stars, directors, sequels and so on.

- Looking at the studios responsible for the top tens, it is easy to see many come from the same 'major' Hollywood studios. Why do you think this is?

- Think about the audiences for the films and the likely certificates given to each (you can find these on the BBFC's website www.bbfc.org.uk). How do you think this relates to box office performance?

RESEARCH TASK

Investigate some of these large studios e.g. Warner Bros, Buena Vista and so on. Do they have, or are they part of, other businesses besides film studios? How would this affect their ability to create and market big-budget films with product tie-ins (think about **ownership**, **multinationals**, **conglomerates** and both **vertical** and **horizontal integration**).

AUDIENCES AND INSTITUTIONS

New Line Cinema

Looking at the tables *The Lord of the Rings* films are the only **New Line Cinema** films in the top tens for any of the three years.

RESEARCH TASK

- Investigate New Line Cinema – what other types films have they produced?

New Line is considered one of the Hollywood 'major independents', like Miramax. Miramax originally were involved in the development of *The Lord of the Rings* but ultimately passed on the project.

TASK

- Find out about Miramax and the types of films they have made. Can you think why they may have passed on making *The Lord of the Rings*?

- Look into the ownership of both New Line and Miramax. They may be 'independent' but are both affiliated to larger studios. As such they are the "independent" arm of bigger companies. Does this still make them independent in your view?

The Lord of the Rings vs. ***Harry Potter***.

If you look at the yearly box office for 2001, and if you cast your mind back, *The Fellowship of the Ring* was very much being hyped against it's 'rival', *Harry Potter and the Philosopher's Stone*. They were considered to have similar audiences.

TASK

- Think about the origins of the two series and the expectations for each. Why were they considered similar do you think?

- Who were the audiences for the two films? Do you think they are similar, or are there differences?

- Would it make a difference that *Harry Potter* was a studio release and *The Lord of the Rings* was an independent? What effect would this have on audiences do you think?

- Can you think why the first *Harry Potter* film was more successful than *The Fellowship...*?

- Now look at the box office for the *Harry Potter/Lord of the Rings* films the following year, in 2002. Why do you think this trend has reversed?

- In 2003 Warner Bros didn't even release a *Harry Potter* film – do you think this was in any way connected to *The Return of the King*?

You may be surprised to learn that New Line Cinema is owned by **TimeWarner**, the company that also own Warner Bros.

- How does this affect your view of the two franchises as rivals? Investigate what **TimeWarner** also own and you will also see how both films had access to other media forms.

AUDIENCES AND INSTITUTIONS

DVD Releases

The Lord of the Rings films had not only an unusual production style, but the way the films were released was also very well-considered and deliberate.

Look at the timeline below of the release of all the instalments of the films:

TIMELINE OF CINEMA AND DVD RELEASES FOR THE LORD OF THE RINGS

The Fellowship of the Ring

- theatrical release 16 December 2001

- DVD release (theatrical, 2 discs) 6 August 2002

- DVD release (extended, 4 discs) 12 November 2002

The Two Towers

- theatrical release 18 December 2002

- DVD release (theatrical, 2 discs) 26 August 2003

- DVD release (extended, 4 discs) 18 November 2003

The Return of the King

- theatrical release 17 December 2003

- DVD release (theatrical, 2 discs) 25 May 2004

- DVD release (extended, 4 discs) 10 December 2004

TASK

- Identify any patterns (time of year and so on). Why do you think the releases were planned this way?

- Consider in more detail the DVD releases:

- What is the purpose, in your opinion, of creating both a 'theatrical' and an 'extended' DVD version of each film?

- What does the release of an 'extended' version say about what audiences want?

- Think about the whole process of going to the cinema and compare it to watching a DVD. What are the main differences?

- It is now acknowledged by the industry that films make more money on DVD sales than in cinemas. Why do you think this is?

Marketing the Films

TASK – Poster Images

- Using the web, look at the key poster art that was used for each of the three films.

- Consider any similarities – colour, images, etc. and what each poster highlights for the audience. Bear in mind that a huge percentage of audiences for Hollywood films are foreign – how do images manage to bridge these barriers and create 'universal appeal'?

- In what way do they represent or show the content of the film in an appealing way? How do they sell the film?

- Is there a 'tagline' (a one-sentence summary to accompany the visuals)?

EXTENSION TASK

You can look at previous trilogy poster art and see if they use any similar patterns – e.g. either or both of the **Star Wars** trilogies, **The Matrix** trilogy, the **Harry Potter** franchise.

TASK – Trailers

Watch one or all of the trailers for the three **The Lord of the Rings** films.

- How does each trailer sell the film?

- What particular narrative elements are highlighted in each?

- Do the trailers stress action sequences, effects, particular characters/stars, or specific generic elements for example?

- Consider the way the trailers are edited – often film trailers use a lot of images in succession (it is easier to see this if the sound is turned off) to create a certain 'feel' for the film, without giving too much away. Consider this in relation to the trailers. How do they generate that all-important 'must-see' factor?

- How similar are the trailers for each film and what do you think the distributors are trying to achieve?

AUDIENCES AND INSTITUTIONS

Fandom and the Internet

'Fans' tend be classed differently from standard moviegoers. Much has been written on the 'niche' appeal of the cult film and how certain audience groups find something personal with which to identify in the work of a particular star, genre or director.

When director Peter Jackson approached the project of **The Lord of the Rings** he knew there were already a lot of fans for the book. One way he addressed any possible backlash against the films being made was to join forces with <u>aintitcoolnews.com</u> asking fans for twenty questions, which he would answer. The response was enormous, and sure enough he answered all the questions. This began a relationship between the film-maker and the fans, made possible only by the internet.

DISCUSSION TASK

- Why is this interesting? Can you think of any other films that have used the internet to appeal to audiences in such a way?

- Consider also the idea of director as auteur (author of a particular film). Think about other 'auteurs' and list them. How accessible are these directors? Did it help or hinder Jackson to be seen as 'approachable' in your opinion?

- What could have happened if Peter Jackson had not consulted these fans, do you think?

TASK

- Go onto a search engine (e.g. <u>www.google.com</u>) and look at how many websites are available for **The Lord of the Rings** films. Have a look at a few – how do they appeal to fans?

- Why do you think the web is used so much by film/music fans?

- One of the main interesting points made about the emergence of the internet in relation to film is that it gives audiences a collective voice and sense of community. Do you agree?

- Think about the different levels of film watching and participation. Do you consider yourself a film fan as it were? How is a fan different from a viewer?

- Look into other websites, for example sites set up for the stars of the films. How do these sites represent fan participation?

EXTENSION TASK

Think about designing your own film news website. After looking at those in existence (<u>aintitcoolnews</u> and <u>darkhorizons</u> for example) how would you create a 'community'?

Gender and Spectatorship

The Lord of the Rings arguably works as a series of films on many levels, for many different audiences.

DISCUSSION TASK

- Who do you think is the biggest audience for *The Lord of the Rings*?

If you look back at the tables of the top ten box office statistics, there is something else to consider in relation to gender. It is often argued that Hollywood cinema appeals most to young men (aged 16-24) and that female audiences are either pigeon-holed in terms of genre (Hollywood targeting them with romantic comedies for example) or must take up a male viewpoint in order to enjoy these films.

Looking back at the tables, choose a selection of films and think about this issue.

- What are the films about?

- Who are the principle characters (are they male or a mixture of male and female?)

- Do you agree or disagree that the films cater for men more than women? Think about some of your favourite films and how you think they address you as a spectator

RESEARCH TASK

Choose a selection of friends or family, some male some female, and show them the tables, asking for the films that appealed the most to their tastes. Then ask them why they liked those particular films, and see if there are any patterns or major differences between male and female audiences.

Now consider *The Lord of the Rings* films. Are the films more 'male' than female or evenly balanced in your view? Again, canvas opinion from friends on family on the films and whether women find them as appealing as men, and if so why?

Two key ways in which audiences find characters appealing is through identification or desire as we touched in when we looked at Narrative.

RESEARCH TASK

Ask your selection of interviewees who they either identify with or desire in *The Lord of the Rings* films.

REPRESENTATION

Gender on Film

- If **The Lord of the Rings** films are set in the 'world of men', where does that leave the female characters – and viewers? Would you argue that the societies represented are **patriarchal**?

The lead females are Arwen (Liv Tyler), Galadriel (Cate Blanchett) and Éowyn (Miranda Otto).

- The former two are some of the biggest 'star' names in the films. Why do you think the female characters are allowed to be played by established stars more than the male characters?

- Does it matter that there are only three female roles of note in the films? Again, ask your selection of interviewees.

Think about the three female characters and their role:

	Character's function?	Costume and appearance?	Love Interest?
Arwen			
Galadriel			
Éowyn			

Gender on Film

It is clear from examining the three female characters that all have similar traits – long hair, flowing ornate costumes, and so on, which are very different to the male characters' functional dress. This could be argued to code them as desirable and romantic princess-like figures rather than active characters in their own right. However each performs some feat or aids a male character in some way:

Arwen: In **_The Fellowship of the Ring_** it is Arwen who rescues Frodo after he has been stabbed, and carries him on horseback to Rivendell.

Galadriel: She is the voice used to narrate the opening of **_The Fellowship of the Ring_**. She is also the donor of gifts that will help Frodo and Sam.

Éowyn: She kills the Witch King in **_The Return of the King_**, the most formidable foe killed by any one character.

DISCUSSION TASK

- What do you think these feats, particularly those of Arwen and Éowyn, mean for female audiences?

- When Éowyn kills the Witch King, she is disguised as a man. What does this mean in terms of **costume** and and traits of **masculinity** and **femininity**? She is the female character most worth studying as she uses a sword and transgresses her role on several occasions.

REPRESENTATION

Oppositional Readings

There is never only one way to interpret events on film. So for example some critics feel Éowyn is a progressive character, others that she in effect has to rid herself of her femininity in order to be active in the story. What these views indicate is that there are different readings available on film. The three most commonly discussed readings are **preferred**, **oppositional** and **negotiated**. **Preferred** is when the audience is led to see events in a certain way (a good example is Tarantino's films when the violence presented is often portrayed as comical – so the way the violence is presented affects our response to it). An **oppositional** reading is where there is an alternative readings available that may contradict this preferred reading (again Tarantino is a good example, an oppositional reading being that he glamorises violence). A **negotiated** reading is just that – a combination of meanings.

In *The Lord of the Rings* there is one storyline that bears particular hallmarks of an oppositional reading. This is the relationship between Frodo and Sam. Whilst they could be argued to be best friends (potentially the preferred reading) they are also at times bonded by a closeness and love that bears more hallmarks of a romance than one may normally find in a big-budget film.

EXTENSION TASK

- Discuss in groups whether you think it is fair to say there is a preferred and an oppositional reading to the relationship between Frodo and Sam. Remember to remain impartial and think about how events are portrayed on film.

- What do you think it means if there are the two readings available?

- If you consider other Hollywood films and their emphasis on heterosexual romance you may see that often any 'oppositional' reading is 'closed down' deliberately. Do you agree and if this is the case why do you think it is so common? You can think about how films reinforce dominant ideology.

- Try and find some other examples where oppositional readings can be found.

Filmography/Bibliography

FILMOGRAPHY

The Lord of the Rings: The Fellowship of the Ring (theatrical/2 disc edition), New Zealand/USA, 2001, 178 minutes

The Lord of the Ring: The Fellowship of the Ring (Special Extended DVD Edition), New Zealand/USA, 2002, 208 minutes

The Lord of the Rings: The Two Towers (theatrical/2 disc edition), 2002, New Zealand/USA, 179 minutes

The Lord of the Rings: The Two Towers (Special Extended DVD Edition), 2003, New Zealand/USA, 223 minutes

The Lord of the Rings: The Return of the King (theatrical/2 disc edition), 2003, New Zealand/USA, 201 minutes

The Lord of the Rings: The Return of the King (Special Extended DVD Edition), New Zealand/USA, 2004, 251 minutes

(NB: The years given for the Special Extended Editions are the years that the DVDs were released.)

Other films by Peter Jackson

Bad Taste, 1987, New Zealand, 89 minutes

Meet the Feebles, 1989, New Zealand, 94 minutes

Brain Dead, 1992, New Zealand, 104 minutes

Heavenly Creatures, 1994, UK/Germany/New Zealand, 99 minutes

The Frighteners, 1996, New Zealand/USA, 110 minutes

King Kong, 2005, New Zealand/USA, 187 minutes

BIBLIOGRAPHY

Bordwell, David and **Thompson, Kristin**, Chapter Four: *Narrative as Formal System in Film Art: An Introduction*, New York: McGraw Hill, 1997

Church-Gibson, Pamela and **Hill, John**, *The Oxford Guide to Film Studies*, Oxford: Oxford University Press, 1998

Cohan, Steve and **Hark, Ina Rae**, *Screening the Male: Exploring Masculinities in Hollywood Cinema*, London: Routledge, 1993

Cook, Pam (ed.), *The Cinema Book*, London: bfi, 1985

Creed, Barbara, *The Monstrous Feminine: Film, Feminism and Psychoanalysis*, London: Routledge, 1993

Doty, Alexander, *Flaming Classics: Queering the Film Canon*, London: Routledge, 2000

Dyer, Richard, *Stars* (revised edn), London: bfi, 1998

Hayward, Susan, *Key Concepts in Cinema Studies* (2nd edn), London: Routledge, 2000

Hollows, Joanne and **Jancovich, Mark**, *Approaches to Popular Film*, Manchester: Manchester University Press, 1995

King, Geoff, *New Hollywood Cinema: An Introduction*, London: I.B.Tauris, 2002

Lusted, David, *The Western*, Harlow: Longman, 2003

Neale, S., 'Masculinity as Spectacle' in **Cohan** and **Hark**, *Screening the Male: Exploring Masculinities in Hollywood Cinema*, London: Routledge, 1993

Neale, S. and **Smith, M.**, *Contemporary Hollywood Cinema*, London: Routledge, 1998

Nelmes, Jill, *An Introduction to Film Studies* (3rd edn), London: Routledge, 2003

Points, Jeremy, *Studying American Beauty*, Leighton Buzzard: Auteur, 2004

Scarratt, Elaine, *Science Fiction Film: A Teacher's Guide*, Leighton Buzzard: Auteur, 2001

Street, Sarah, *Costume and Cinema: Dress Codes in Popular Film*, London: Wallflower, 2001

Stringer, Julian (ed.), *Movie Blockbusters*, London: Routledge, 2003

Tasker, Yvonne, *Spectacular Bodies: Gender, Genre and the Action Cinema*, London: Comedia, 2003

Tasker, Yvonne., (ed.), *Action and Adventure Cinema*, London: Routledge, 2004

Turner, Graham, *Film as Social Practice* (2nd edn), London: Routledge, 1993

Articles

Brooks, Xan, 'The Ring Cycle', *The Observer*, 7 December 2001

Fuller, Graham, 'Kingdom Come', *Film Comment*, Jan/Feb 2004

Mulvey, Laura, 'Visual Pleasure and Narrative Cinema' in *Screen*, Vol. 16, Pt. 3, 1975

Merritt, Stephanie, 'No Sex Please, We're Hobbits', *The Observer*, 7 December 2003

Screen International, 4 January 2002

Shefrin, E., 'Lord of the Rings, Star Wars and Mapping Participatory Fandom', *Critical Studies in Media Communication*, Vol. 21 No. 3, 2004

Spaulding, Jeremy, 'The Tail Wagging the Dog', *Film Comment*, March/April 2004

Spencer, Neil, 'Mordor, He Wrote', *The Observer*, 9 December, 2001

Guides

Smith, Jim and **Matthews, J. Clive**, *The Lord of the Rings: The Films, the Books and the Radio Series*, London: Virgin Books, 2004

The Rough Guide Lord of the Rings, London: Haymarket, 2003

Websites

There are inevitably countless websites dedicated to the films and the books. These can be found through Google. The official film site is at www.thelordoftherings.net. Also worth looking at for statistical and production information is the Internet Movie Database, www.imdb.com.